GREAT LIVES OBSERVED

Gerald Emanuel Stearn, *General Editor*

EACH VOLUME IN THE SERIES VIEWS THE CHARACTER AND ACHIEVE-
MENT OF A GREAT WORLD FIGURE IN THREE PERSPECTIVES—
THROUGH HIS OWN WORDS, THROUGH THE OPINIONS OF HIS CON-
TEMPORARIES, AND THROUGH RETROSPECTIVE JUDGMENTS—THUS
COMBINING THE INTIMACY OF AUTOBIOGRAPHY, THE IMMEDIACY
OF EYE-WITNESS OBSERVATION, AND THE OBJECTIVITY OF MODERN
SCHOLARSHIP.

GERALD D. NASH, *the editor of this volume in the Great
Lives Observed series, is Associate Professor of History at the
University of New Mexico. He is a frequent contributor to
many scholarly history journals and is the author of* State
Government and Economic Development *as well as the editor
of* Issues in American Economic History.

Forthcoming volumes in the Great Lives Observed series

Elizabeth I, edited by Joseph Levine

John Calhoun, edited by Margaret L. Coit

Hitler, edited by George Stein

Lincoln, edited by James P. Shenton

Lloyd George, edited by Martin Gilbert

Luther, edited by Paul A. Lee

Mao, edited by Jerome Ch'en

GREAT LIVES OBSERVED

Franklin Delano
Roosevelt

Edited by GERALD D. NASH

The masses of mankind . . . knew
that he was asking the right questions,
and if he did not always find the right answers,
someone, who had learned what to look for,
eventually would.

—WALTER LIPPMANN

PRENTICE-HALL, INC., ENGLEWOOD CLIFFS, N. J.

Contents

PART ONE
FDR HIMSELF

1
Before the White House   13

FDR at Harvard, *14*   New York State Senator, *16*   Assistant Secretary of the Navy, *19*   Polio, *21*   Statesman: Commonwealth Club Address, *24*

2
The Presidency   31

The New President: The First Inaugural, *31*   The Great Experimenter: Fireside Chat Amidst the First Hundred Days, *34* Business: The NRA, *39*   Unemployment, *42*   Regional Development: The TVA, *43*   Social Security, *46*   The New Deal Renewed, *47*   The Negro, *51*   Battle with the Supreme Court: Fireside Chat of 1937, *52*   Diplomatist: Good Neighbor, *58* Quarantine of Foreign Aggressors, *61*   Lend-Lease Press Conference, December 17, 1940, *65*   Yalta: Roosevelt at War, *68*

PART TWO
FDR OBSERVED

3
FDR's First Fifty Years   71

Sara Delano Roosevelt: Childhood, *72*   Endicott Peabody: Groton, *73*   James Roosevelt: Harvard, *74*   Eleanor Roose-

GREAT LIVES OBSERVED

ROOSEVELT

Introduction

Historians have written of the Age of Pericles and of Alexander, of Leonardo and Napoleon, and of Jefferson and Jackson. Lately they have also begun to designate the period of the New Deal and World War II in the U.S. as the Age of Roosevelt. Why do they identify an entire era with a great personality? Perhaps it is because in all recorded history the faiths men lived by—their ideals, hopes and values—were often crystallized in the thoughts and actions of great individuals.

But how is greatness to be judged? An outstanding man, concluded Sidney Hook in *The Hero in History*, is an individual to whom we can attribute preponderant influence in determining events which would have been very different without his actions. His importance may be fortuitous in relation to events, in the sense that only because of his presence at a certain time and place in history is he allowed to influence a sequence of happenings. Or, he may be significant because he is *event-making*, that is, by dint of outstanding traits of character or intelligence he is able to affect a pattern of events. In short, the times may make the man, but the man may also mold the times. In outstanding careers both of these circumstances have usually combined to produce greatness. One criterion of historical greatness, then, is the degree in which an individual has affected the course of the lives of not only millions of his contemporaries but also of many generations thereafter.

Measured by this standard, Franklin Delano Roosevelt clearly is one of the great men of the twentieth century. Large numbers of peoples both within and without the United States were affected by his actions in his years of public office (1928-1945), and his policies have not yet run their full course. Although FDR left the stamp of his personality everywhere during his Presidential tenure, yet he also reflected many important characteristics of his own age. There was a subtle blend in him of personal traits with characteristic features of the period, a blend which proved to be a springboard to eminence. How did this combination bring him distinction?

Certainly there was little in FDR's early life to indicate that he would achieve greatness. Born in 1882 in Hyde Park, New York, at the estate of an old and well established patrician family, he was the only child of John and Sara Delano Roosevelt. His father was a well-to-do although not opulent middle-aged country gentleman; his mother was a well-born daughter of the Delano clan.

1

As an only child, the young Roosevelt led a somewhat cloistered and well protected life during his first fourteen years. He was raised largely by his doting mother and a succession of admiring governesses, and he grew up in a small and well-ordered world. His family took him on frequent trips to Europe, and they spent their summers at Campobello, Maine. There FDR developed a deep and lifelong love for the sea. By the time he was ten years old, he had his own sailboat and was developing considerable nautical skill. Even during the winters at Hyde Park he was provided with opportunities for an active and interesting outdoor life. The happy world of his childhood is well revealed by the reminiscences of his mother, and by other contemporaries. Later Roosevelt biographies, such as Frank Freidel, have examined FDR's early environment in considerable detail, and concluded that such an upbringing was not unusual for boys of his social background.

FDR's vistas were widened in 1896 when his parents reluctantly sent him to Groton, a new Massachusetts preparatory school for sons of the wealthy. Conducted by its founder and headmaster, Endicott Peabody, the central purpose of the school's training was the building of character. Peabody also hoped to inculcate in his students the ideal of service to one's fellow man. FDR's career at Groton was not outstanding, but it is clear that he adjusted rather easily to a new routine in his life which was considerably different from his upbringing as an only child. His letters of this period show that within a few months he felt himself accepted by the society of adolescents into which he was thrown. He was not subjected to cruel hazing which the students inflicted upon those who ignored local etiquette, or who in some small way failed to conform to the judgment of the group. FDR's adaptability was also noted by headmaster Peabody in later years when he looked back on the record of his most distinguished graduate. And the biographer, Frank Freidel, has found additional evidence to indicate that FDR showed great flexibility in settling into the preparatory school routine at Groton.

Like most of his classmates, FDR went on to Harvard in 1900, where he spent the next four years very enjoyably. His college career was devoted not so much to serious study as to a wide range of social and extracurricular activities. To be sure, he worked at least enough to maintain a "gentleman's" average. Moreover, in his senior year he was chosen editor of the *Crimson,* the Harvard newspaper, a position which brought him great prestige on campus. His own writings of this period indicate that his interests were largely restricted to the affairs of his social group and of the college. Altogether, his record at Harvard was not exceptional. Later biographers were to decide, however, that his varied non-academic activities added to his poise and to his sense of social status, and resulted in a social affability which was to stand him in good stead when he entered politics.

Much to his mother's dismay, FDR's graduation from Harvard was followed in 1905 by his marriage to Anna Eleanor Roosevelt, his fifth cousin. A shy and withdrawn young woman, Eleanor Roosevelt brought both a new seriousness and a new social awareness into FDR's life. The marriage ceremony in New York City was one of the gala social events of the season particularly since Eleanor's uncle—and Franklin's distant cousin—was the President of the United States, Theodore Roosevelt, who insisted on giving away the bride. Sara Delano Roosevelt was not overjoyed about that "other woman" in her son's life and soon attempted to dominate the young couple. She could do this in part because she controlled her deceased husband's estate, which FDR depended upon for his living expenses.

After returning from a honeymoon in Europe, FDR settled down in New York City where he attended Columbia University's law school for two years. Although he never graduated—for it seems that legal studies bored him—he was admitted to the New York State Bar after passing the required examination. Between 1907 and 1910 he served in the distinguished New York law firm of Carter, Ledyard and Milburn, but found little real satisfaction in his work.

Under the strong influence of Theodore Roosevelt, the young FDR decided in 1910 to enter politics. From the very beginning of his public career FDR was oriented toward reform. With a magnetic name and great social prestige, he was able to attract the support of local Democratic leaders in Dutchess County (in upstate New York), and secured the nomination for a New York State Senate seat. Campaigning in a traditionally Republican district, he traveled about in a striking red automobile and conducted a strenuous speaking tour. His personal charm was already manifest on these occasions, as well as his ability to talk effectively with people in various walks of life. Many of the farmers in the district were won over by his promises of reform, and by his challenge of Tammany Hall, New York City's political machine. When the votes were counted he found himself elected, the first Democrat in the State Senate from the district in half a century.

FDR became a leader of the Reform Democrats in the New York legislature between 1911 and 1913. His speeches of that period reveal his progressive tendencies. Contemporary observers were impressed by this new Roosevelt—as newspaper reports clearly indicate—but few expected him to measure up to his more famous namesake. The importance of FDR's legislative experience could not, of course, be evaluated in 1912, but later biographers such as Freidel have discovered and emphasized its significance: the young patrician was impressed with the need for legislative compromise.

If Theodore Roosevelt was one of FDR's political idols, Woodrow Wilson was another. During the presidential campaign of 1912 FDR worked actively for the Democratic ticket headed by Wilson. As a reward, in 1913 the new President appointed him Assistant Secretary of the Navy, a position once held by Theodore Roosevelt, and one which FDR with his love for the sea accepted with great relish.

During the next seven years he gained valuable political and administrative experience in this post. His responsibilities included management of the Navy's shipyards, and the conduct of the Department's labor relations. His letters during these years reveal how absorbed he was with this work. They also reflect his huge enjoyment of public life. His coworkers and superiors were impressed by his good looks, his charm, his winning personality and his capable performance as a junior member of the Administration. His immediate chief, Secretary of the Navy Josephus Daniels, became greatly enamored with his assistant and prophesied that he would one day occupy the White House. Historians have dwelt upon the remarks of FDR's contemporaries about him during World War I. They have concluded that his war-time service provided valuable administrative experience, while Wilsonian progressivism left a deep imprint upon the reform-minded young New Yorker.

Roosevelt's success in the Navy Department, his residence in a large and populous state such as New York, and his prominent name all combined to lead Governor James M. Cox of Ohio, the Democratic Presidential standard-bearer in 1920, to choose FDR as his Vice-Presidential running mate. FDR embarked on an extensive campaign and showed considerable abilities as a public speaker. Even if the race was unsuccessful, the campaign made him a national figure. Many contemporaries remarked on the maturing effect which this experience had upon FDR, a conclusion that is confirmed by later historians.

A promising political career was apparently cut short in 1921 when FDR fell ill with polio. During the next half dozen years he was preoccupied with efforts to walk again and to regain his health. This period of confinement had its effect on the former sportsman and athlete who was now cruelly crippled. He not only found more time for reflection without distractions, but he was also thrown back upon his inner resources. The crisis brought out a new seriousness in his character, as well as humility and added maturity. His writings during the illness reveal determination and courage, while his wife and other contemporaries commented upon his great fortitude and optimism.

Largely as a result of the urgings of his wife, of his close confidant, Louis M. Howe, and of political leaders like Al Smith, FDR considered reentering public life. In 1928 he ran successfully for the governorship of New York—at the same time that Smith lost to Herbert Hoover in the Presidential race. Reelected in 1930, FDR embarked upon a vigorous and far ranging reform program for New York. During this period he became concerned with social welfare, labor legislation, public power, judicial and administrative reorganization, and increasingly, with unemployment. But if some political observers were greatly impressed with his performance, others—Walter Lippmann, for example—still had doubts. Historians have viewed his gubernatorial policies as experiments leading to the New Deal on the national level. They provided an opportunity to test certain purported remedies against the depression, and they brought FDR into contact with an able group of planners and administrators, such as Harry Hopkins, Frances Perkins, A. A. Berle, Raymond Moley, and others.

FDR's election to the Presidency in 1932 was as much a personal triumph as it was a national repudiation of the Hoover Administration. Even if FDR had no coherent, well-thought-out plan to meet the difficulties of the depression, yet he did have certain broad goals in mind, which some of his campaign speeches in 1932, particularly the famous Commonwealth address, revealed clearly. Above all, he had a willingness to experiment, to try new remedies in dealing with the economic crisis. This was reflected in many of his speeches and writings during the New Deal. His pragmatism—fortified with a strong dose of optimism—appealed to millions of Americans during these grim years. One of FDR's prime contributions in the 1930's, according to some contemporaries and later critics, was the revitalization of the spirit of the American people.

FDR's first New Deal policies largely emphasized the solution of problems resulting from the economic crisis, and were intended primarily to provide relief and to promote economic recovery. His Inaugural Address —while in no way underestimating the seriousness of the depression for the whole nation—breathed a spirit of buoyant hope and optimism, and urged Americans not to despair even if there were no quick solutions for the existing difficulties. During FDR's first hundred days in the White House, Congress enacted a surprisingly large number of his legislative recommendations. In rapid succession FDR and the lawmakers created several new federal organizations: the Federal Emergency Relief Administration, which extended aid directly to the jobless; the Agricultural Adjustment Act which stabilized agriculture by controls over production and distribution; and the National Recovery Administration, which aided business. In the hope that federally sponsored regional power development programs would stimulate recovery, FDR enthusiastically approved of the creation of the Tennessee Valley Authority, which Senator George Norris of Nebraska had been advocating for more than a decade. Financial reforms included certain banking restrictions and the establishment of the Securities and Exchange Commission which was to supervise the issue of stocks and bonds by private corporations.

In 1935, however, FDR launched a second New Deal which emphasized reform rather than relief and recovery. Perhaps the chief executive took this step not altogether willingly, and was responding to the pressure of dissident groups on the Right and Left. In any event, ex-President Hoover and his followers were becoming increasingly vociferous—they charged that FDR was developing into an autocrat. Disenchanted businessmen formed groups, such as the American Liberty League, and attracted the support of some embittered political moderates, like Al Smith, who simply hated Roosevelt. At the same time, others complained that FDR was neither doing enough to help the masses nor to overcome the depression. Perhaps the most vocal of these dissenters was Senator Huey P. Long of Louisiana, founder of the Share-the-Wealth movement, which was attracting a considerable following. Hardly less effective was the popular radio priest, Father Charles E. Coughlin, who was urging FDR to make drastic monetary reforms. Meanwhile, Earl Browder and the American Communist Party were condemning FDR and his New Deal completely. As the national elections of 1936 approached, the pressure from these groups of the Left and the Right led FDR to embark on a number of important new reforms.

The second New Deal thus embraced a wide range of reform legislation as a consequence of widespread political discussion. One of the most important acts during this period was the enactment of the Social Security law in 1935. No less important was the Wagner Labor Relations Act during the same year, which guaranteed unions the right to practice collective bargaining. Other important measures in 1935 were the Banking Act, the Public Utility Holding Act, the Motor Carrier Act, and the Revenue Act, which increased the tax burdens on large corporations.

The reform program was interrupted by FDR's battle with the United States Supreme Court early in his second term. In a series of important decisions, a divided Court nullified more than a dozen significant New Deal laws. Flushed by his tremendous victory at the polls in 1936, FDR entered upon his famous "Supreme Court Packing Plan." He proposed to enlarge the Court and to compel the retirement of judges past the age of seventy so that he could appoint justices of his own political persuasion. These proposals aroused such a storm of protest, however, even among many of the President's staunch supporters, that he was forced to drop them. But if he lost the battle, he won the war, for after 1937 the Supreme Court came to view New Deal legislation in a more favorable light.

Nonetheless, the scars left by this battle slowed the progress of reform. The severe economic recession of 1937 showed that FDR had by no means solved many major problems. Thus, between 1937 and 1939, the President and Congress embarked on another round of legislation to pull the country out of economic crisis. This included the Bankhead-Jones Farm Tenancy Act, the Wagner-Steagall Housing Act, the creation of a second AAA, the Fair Labor Standards Act, and the administrative reorganization of certain executive departments. These concluded most of the New

Deal reform measures, for after 1939 FDR increasingly concentrated his attention on foreign policies.

Even before that time, however, the rise of Germany and Japan as expansionist powers had led FDR to adjust American policies to new world conditions. In his first term the President sought to realize an avowed goal of becoming a "good neighbor" to all other nations. This policy was implemented by United States recognition of Soviet Russia in 1933, and especially by the development of closer relationships with Latin American nations. The Reciprocal Trade Agreements Act of 1934 was a major step in this direction. But the Germans' remilitarization of the Rhineland, Mussolini's invasion of Ethiopia, and joint German-Italian intervention in the Spanish Civil War after 1936, followed by the Japanese invasion of China in 1937, further complicated America's position in international affairs. Clearly, some change of policy was needed.

FDR responded by urging a policy of national defense at home, and a "quarantine" of aggressors abroad, as he called it, in his famous speech of October 5, 1937. During the next four years, in one way or another, the President sought to implement these policies while maintaining American neutrality. When the German invasion of Poland in September, 1939, inaugurated World War II in Europe, and the Nazi-Soviet pact of that year clearly posed a threat to the democracies, FDR increased his efforts to knit closer ties with France and England. However, the fall of France in June, 1940, and the Germans' occupation of both the Low Countries and of northern Europe greatly narrowed the President's choice of action.

Henceforth, FDR emphasized the principle of collective security in his diplomacy. Large-scale American aid to Great Britain became an important part of this policy, to which the President added a personal dimension by meeting frequently with the British Prime Minister, Winston Churchill. Perhaps their most famous conference came on board ship in the Atlantic during August, 1941, where the two statesmen promulgated the Atlantic Charter, a statement of joint aims for a post-war world. Meanwhile, FDR had inaugurated the Lend-Lease program in January of that year. Lend-Lease was the agreement by which the United States sent needed war matériel and supplies to England, in return for leases on military bases located in British possessions in America. Ultimately Congress authorized more than seven billion dollars for this program. The President also used his executive authority to transfer to Great Britain fifty outmoded American destroyers which were desperately needed for convoy duty. During 1941, when German submarines were attacking United States vessels in the Atlantic, neutrality became increasingly unrealistic. On December 7, 1941, the Japanese attack on Pearl Harbor precipitated American entrance into World War II, effectively ending the neutrality policy.

FDR now assumed the new role of commander-in-chief of American forces, and became a leader of the Allied forces as well. In this capacity he provided general direction for almost every phase of the war effort. Much of his time was devoted to diplomacy, however, and to cementing the Grand Alliance. Since FDR's political "style" favored personal contact, he embarked on a series of war-time conferences with America's allies to implement battle plans as well as peace aims. Thus, in January, 1943, he met with Churchill in North Africa—at the Casablanca Conference—to plan the Allied invasion of North Africa and Italy. In November of that year both men journeyed to Cairo to discuss Far Eastern problems with the Nationalist Chinese leader, General Chiang Kai Shek, while FDR met Premier Stalin of Russia for the first time in Teheran. There FDR and Stalin agreed on the eventual opening of a second front in Europe. The final conference which also signified the high point of Allied unity, came near the end of the war when the "Big Three"—Roosevelt, Churchill and Stalin—met in the Crimea at the resort of Yalta. There they discussed proposed peace settlements for both Europe and the Far East. Now that a victory over the Axis powers seemed not too far distant, they sought to work out some of their differences involving the United Nations, boundaries in Poland and eastern Europe, and the defeat of Japan in the Far East. The Yalta Agreements which FDR brought back to the United States in March, 1945, aroused an almost immediate controversy and led to months of serious debate. To regain his strength FDR journeyed in early April of 1945 to Warm Springs, Georgia, his favorite vacation retreat. There, on the afternoon of April 12, 1945, he suddenly remarked to his secretary: "I've got a terrific headache." Then he slumped over, the victim of a cerebral hemorrhage. A great life had ended, but not his achievements nor his influence on succeeding generations.

A complex personality, perhaps no one knew FDR well. Even those who were in daily contact with him were unable to fathom him completely. And if it was difficult for contemporaries, it is even harder for those who did not know him while he was alive. Some measure of his character can be obtained, however, from his own writings, from the varied reports of contemporaries, and from the work of biographers who have tried to probe deeply into his life.

Most of these students of FDR agree that a pragmatic attitude was one of his outstanding traits. Already as a school boy his ability to adapt to a wide range of situations was notable. His experiences as a legislator and as Assistant Secretary of the Navy further developed this flexibility. When he was Chief Executive his openness to suggestions and his willingness to try new remedies or ideas became distinguishing features of his "style" as a statesman and politician. He tended to shrug off abstract concepts, and instead preferred to deal with immediate and concrete issues. Although he was at ease in the company of intellectuals he was not one of them himself. Not bound by any dogma or theory, he felt free to experiment with all ideas that seemed relevant to the solution of pressing problems. In many ways FDR also reflected the qualities of the American aristocrat. His awareness of his social status bred a sense of security in him not often found in men of less fortunate background. Like Theodore Roosevelt, FDR had a sense of *noblesse oblige*. When this was infused with a definite strain of moralism derived from a Puritan (Dutch Reform) heritage, it resulted in a strong sense of responsibility, or even the idea of "stewardship." Thus, it was given to the leaders of American society to take the initiative in righting obvious wrongs, whether these involved the undue concentration of wealth, social ills, or political corruption. And, like his political mentors, Theodore Roosevelt and Woodrow Wilson, FDR also possessed a strong sense of morality, a feeling which had been assiduously developed by Headmaster Peabody at Groton.

To such characteristics largely derived from his background, FDR added unique personal qualities. If he lacked depth of thought, yet he had considerable breadth. His range of interests, and his curiosity was extremely wide, and he was well read in many fields, including American history and lore. His retentive mind absorbed a great deal of information, more often from personal contacts with others than from books. To be sure, his knowledge was eclectic rather than original and profound. But he had an uncanny knack for picking up ideas, for selecting concepts and suggestions presented to him by experts in diverse fields, and then combining in a meaningful fashion what often appeared to be odds and ends in his own peculiar synthesis.

Much of FDR's effectiveness was due to his great skill in communication. Few Presidents have been more adept in explaining complex issues in simple language to laymen. Better than any of his advisers or speech writers, he had an intuitive feeling for what the average person could comprehend. In addition, he was gifted with one of the most effective radio voices of his generation. Such qualities enabled him to "chat" with millions of Americans with an intimacy and personal quality not attained by his predecessors. As the White House mail attested, large numbers of men and women considered him to be their own, particular friend, who had a full and sympathetic understanding of their individual problems.

If FDR was able to project an image as an understanding and kindly man, it was not pure contrivance, for he had a genuine sympathy for suffering humanity. Perhaps it was largely derived from his struggle with polio; possibly the disease developed a stronger sense of compassion within him. But his concern for the welfare of others was often apparent in his public actions and explains why he was widely loved and admired.

By instinct, training, and experience FDR was also a consummate politician. To contemporaries and later historians alike it appeared that he had mastered most of the skills needed in American politics. His particular style was often imitated, but rarely duplicated. It was based in part upon his personal charm, for he could be as disarming with individuals as with crowds. Moreover, and in contrast to Herbert Hoover, he was able to generate personal attachment in individuals at every level of intelligence. In addition, he was a superb manipulator of power. By creating tensions among his subordinates he was often able to bring out their most constructive impulses. Yet he always retained for himself the ultimate authority and choice. Another political asset was his ability to compromise, for he always seemed willing to trade some immediate issue for the attainment of his larger and long-range goals. To idealists, and to some doctrinaire liberals, this tendency often seemed to be cynical opportunism. But FDR's sense of timing—another instrument in his politician's kit—was accurate more often than not. Usually he had a "feel" for the proper occasion on which to apply pressure, to cajole, or to retreat. In combination with each other, these skills made him one of the master politicians of his day.

No man is without weaknesses, and FDR had his share. Most frequently, contemporaries accused him of a lack of candor, if not outright dishonesty. With a great desire to please, FDR rarely told his listeners, even his closest associates, what he really thought. He also could not bear to confront close associates with unwelcome news—perhaps that they were of no further use to him—and consequently often straddled knotty issues without taking decisive action. These characteristics were expressed in small actions as well as large. Critics, such as Charles A. Beard, charged, for example, that FDR's pronouncements on American neutrality between 1935 and 1941 were deceptive, since the President at the same time was preparing the nation for participation in the war.

Other observers detected a streak of impulsiveness in FDR, which could lead to irresponsibility. While his close confidant, Louis M. Howe, was alive, he sought to keep FDR's impulsiveness in check. But it was especially the critics of the Yalta Agreements in 1945 who charged that FDR's irresponsibility was at its height when he impulsively trusted the word of Joseph Stalin, despite official intelligence reports which suggested that it would be desirable to doubt Soviet pledges.

The literature concerning FDR is likely to grow in future years because the policies for which he stood, the actions for which he was responsible, and the values which he symbolized continue to affect the American people during the second half of the twentieth century. Thus, a knowledge of FDR's motives, his goals, and his achievements is essential not only for an understanding of the New Deal era, but for an understanding of our own. The selections that follow—from FDR himself, from those who knew him, and from those who have made a detailed study of his life—should aid in providing criteria by which to judge one of the most interesting personalities in modern times.

Chronology of the Life of Franklin Delano Roosevelt

1882	(January 30) Born in Hyde Park, New York, son of John and Sara Delano Roosevelt.
1882-1896	Education at home by private tutors.
1896	Begins studies at Groton School, Groton, Massachusetts, under Headmaster Endicott Peabody.
1900	Enters Harvard.
1904	Editor of Harvard *Crimson;* B.A. degree.
1904	Begins studies at Columbia University Law School.
1905	Marriage to Anna Eleanor Roosevelt, FDR's fifth cousin.
1906	Begins practice in law offices of Carter, Ledyard and Milburn, New York City.
1911	Enters New York State Senate (Democrat).
1913-1920	Assistant Secretary of the Navy.
1914	Unsuccessful effort to secure Democratic nomination in New York for U.S. Senate.
1918	Visits European battlefronts.
1920	Vice-Presidential candidate of Democratic Party.
1921	Attack of polio.
1921-1924	Convalescence and semi-retirement.
1924	Reenters public life by nominating Al Smith for President at Democratic Presidential Convention.
1924-1928	Recuperation at Warm Springs, Georgia, and Hyde Park, New York.
1928-1932	Governor of New York State.
1932	Elected President of the United States on promise of a New Deal.
1933	Inaugurates first New Deal.
1933	(March) Declares Bank Holiday. (March-June) First Hundred Days; establishes NRA, AAA, SEC, TVA with Congressional approval.
1933	(July 3) Bombshell Message to London Economic Conference.
1934	Promotes Reciprocal Trade Agreements Act. Fosters Good Neighbor policy.
1935	Shift to second New Deal and reform (Social Security Act, Wagner Labor Relations Act, WPA, Federal Power Act, Public Utility Holding Act).
1936	Elected to second term with landslide victory.

1937	Advocates Supreme Court "Packing Plan."
	Economic Recession.
	(October 5) "Quarantine" Speech.
1938	Second AAA, Fair Labor Standards Act.
	Urges world peace and sends appeal to Hitler at Munich Conference.
1939	Urges U.S. rearmament for national defense;
	supports peace-time draft.
1940	Advocates increased preparedness.
	Reelected to third term.
1941	Develops Lend-Lease program of aid to Great Britain;
	negotiates destroyer deal; signs Atlantic Charter after meeting
	with British Prime Minister Winston Churchill.
1941	(December 7) Japanese attack on Pearl Harbor.
	FDR urges Congress to declare war on Japan and Germany.
1943	Meets Churchill at Casablanca to plan war strategy,
	other meetings in Washington and Quebec.
	Meets Churchill and Chiang Kai-Shek at Cairo;
	meets Premier Joseph Stalin at Teheran to discuss joint policies
	and a second front.
1944	Elected to a fourth term.
1945	Journeys to Yalta for conference with Churchill and Stalin
	on plans for peace.
1945	(April 12) Death by cerebral hemorrhage at Warm Springs, Georgia.

PART ONE

FDR HIMSELF

*What qualities of mind and character did FDR reveal as
a youth, and how was he shaped by the experiences of his early
life? Some understanding of his motives, his ideals, his values, and
his successes can be gathered from his own writings. Those from the
period prior to his first term in the Presidency (1933-1936) reveal an
able but not an extraordinary man, a patrician who by dint of the
proper family background and a charming personality was able to
gain a succession of public offices. By 1932 he was a prominent politician, but one of whom only few expected greatness. The demands
of the Presidency, however, brought out unusual qualities of leadership in FDR. He showed this development in domestic and foreign
policies as well as in the coordination of civil and military affairs
during World War II. The excerpts from FDR's letters and speeches
in Part One are designed to illustrate the gradual development of
maturity and increasing stature in FDR during the various stages
of his career.*

1

Before the White House

*It can be said that FDR spent half a century in preparing
for the Presidency. During this period he revealed many of the
characteristics of an upper-class background. His interests, his poise,
his confidence of status, and his acceptance of the concept of stewardship—that is, a concern for the less fortunate—all were typical:
he was a responsible scion of America's old and well established
families. His youthful letters from Harvard provide a glimpse of the
social world in which he lived. But to these important elements of
his heritage he added personal qualities which increasingly lifted
him above the level of more ordinary men with similar upbringing.
His pragmatism and extraordinary adaptability were already evident in his early life although he developed these traits more fully
later. Combined with personal attractiveness and charm, a buoyant
optimism, and an acute sense of timing, these characteristics prom-*

13

ised success in a variety of roles. The range of his qualifications for elective office is reflected in the following selections from his writings, which are drawn from his letters and speeches while in private life and then as a public official from 1910 until his election to the Presidency in 1932.

FDR AT HARVARD

CAMBRIDGE
Oct. 5, 1900,
Friday.

My dearest Mama & Papa,

I have such a lot to write about that I don't quite know where to begin. But to go back to Monday— In the afternoon the first foot-ball practice with a long run made us stiff, but after supper the fun began. Most of the Groton, St. M., & St. Pauls & Pomfret fellows were in at Sanborn's, and last night I visited the Lords. The curtains haven't come but I am writing J.&M. Paine will send the rug for my room in a few days. I am pretty well unpacked tho' no pictures are hung yet. There are still over 100 candidates for the '04 team & I shan't make it but possibly a scrub team. I am crazy for a picture of Tip.

No more now. Will write Sunday. I lunch at Sturgises then.

Ever with lots of love your affec son

F.D.R.[1]

CAMBRIDGE
Oct. 14, 1900,
Sunday.

My dearest Mama & Papa

How perfectly delighted I was to get your letter saying that you intended to come on to Boston next Sunday! I can hardly wait until the day, and I shall be at the Union Station at 3 to meet you. I will get five seats at the Theatre & ask 3 boys to dinner. I don't know whether you intend to go to the Touraine or the Somerset, but I fancy it will be the Touraine.

I have just got back from Groton, but I must go back to the beginning. I went up on Friday at 3 p.m., and that evening about 20 graduates only came. On Saturday morning about 200 people arrived and the Consecra-

[1] Elliot Roosevelt, *FDR: His Personal Letters: Early Years* (New York, 1947), pp. 425-426.

tion Service began at 11:30. The graduates marched by forms to the Chapel, the original form consisting of 1 grad. The service was most impressive, there were 50 clergy in their robes, & the Chapel had 400 persons in it, on chairs, camp-stools, etc, it was an event which none of us will ever forget. After the service there was a big stand up lunch in the dining-room, and in the afternoon a foot-ball game with Hopkinson which Groton won, 6-0.

Last Wednesday I had received an invitation from Mr. Higley to spend Sunday with him so I moved over to his house (also Warren Motley) on Saturday & had a most delightful visit there, away from the awful crowd at the school. There was a grand dinner at the School in the evening & speeches & songs afterwards. Today there was Communion & the regular services, & I came back tonight at 7 o'clock. When you come, please bring my new pipe (Uncle Ned's) as it was forgotten when I packed. I am not smoking as I am in training for foot-ball.

No more now. Will write on Tuesday.

Ever with lots of love your affec son

FRANKLIN.[2]

THE HARVARD CRIMSON
JAN. 12, 1904,
Tuesday.

Dearest Mama—

I wrote you last week and found the scribble in my pocket today— Positively I am the most intelligent man in Harvard without exception! Now I must confess— On Saturday I found I had no engagement & went to N.Y. on the 10 o'clock— E. & I had a quiet evening & went to Church together on Sunday— I lunched at the Parishes' & came on here again on the 3 o'clock getting here at 10, just in time to write my editorial. You know I positively couldn't help it— There was nothing to keep me here and I knew I should be in a much better humor for a short trip to N.Y.!

Last week I dined at the Quincy's, the Amory's & the Thayer's, three as high-life places as are to be found in blue-blooded, blue stockinged, bean eating Boston!

Many thanks for the Tuxedo & gloves & smoking apparatus. I have been up every night till all hours, but am doing a little studying, a little riding & a few party calls. It is dreadfully hard to be a student, a society whirler, a "prominent & democratic fellow," & a fiancé all at the same time

² Ibid, p. 427.

—but it [is] worth while, especially the last & next year, tho' hard will be easier— I may go to N.Y. on the 1 o'clock on Friday & hope to find you there on arrival— You will surely stay over Sunday—won't you please—we have so much to talk over about the trip etc.

Your devoted

FDR.[3]

NEW YORK STATE SENATOR

After college and his marriage in 1905, FDR studied for two years at Columbia University's law school and then worked for a time in the distinguished New York law firm of Carter, Ledyard and Milburn. By 1910, however, he had made up his mind to enter politics and won a seat in the New York State Senate as a Democrat from Dutchess County. From the day that he entered the legislature he cut a dashing figure. He greatly enjoyed the limelight. There he early identified himself with the reformers. He opposed Tammany Hall, New York City's powerful political machine, and supported progressive measures. His reform sentiments were clearly articulated in a speech which he delivered at Troy, New York on March 3, 1912.

. . . If we go back through history, or rather through the history of the past thousand years, we are struck by the fact that as a general proposition the Aryan races have been struggling to obtain individual freedom. For nearly one thousand years and in almost every European and American country this has been the great and fundamental question in the economic life of the people. The Reformation, for instance, and the Renaissance in Europe are too commonly regarded as religious or educational struggles and have not, by teachers of history, been sufficiently explained as efforts on the part of the various peoples affected to obtain individual liberty. In the same way the American revolution, the French revolution and at a later date the general European uprisings of 1848.

Almost every struggle of representative government has been in reality an attempt to secure individual freedom and almost everywhere one turns today, can be found a form of government, which to a great degree, guarantees this personal liberty. There are exceptions of course, like Russia. It is a sweeping statement to make but taking the nations as a whole

[3] *Ibid,* p. 523.

today, in Europe and America, the liberty of the individual has been accomplished.

On my assumption that this liberty of the individual has been largely accomplished and that it has been until now the main object of human research, I come to the next step in the search for the cause of the conditions of unrest today, and I find the cause in the growth of what is in modern civilization a new way of looking at things, a new economic theory. It is new because there never has been any immediate need for such a theory in the past. When men are serfs or are ruled by tyrants they need first of all, individual freedom. They do not need to go beyond that, but when this freedom has been acquired they have not yet got to Utopia.

During the past century we have acquired a new set of conditions which we must seek to solve. To put it in the simplest and fewest words I have called this new theory the struggle for liberty of the community rather than liberty of the individual. When all is said and done every new doctrine which had been advanced for the last fifty years comes under this definition. Every new star that people have hitched their wagon to for the past half century, whether it be anti-rebating, or anti-trusts, or new fashioned education, or conservation of our natural resources or State regulation of common carriers, or commission government, or any of the thousand and one other things that we have run after of late, almost without any exception come under the same heading. They are all steps in the evolution of the new theory of the liberty of the community.

The Socialist has at times called this same thing 'community interest' and some high-sounding orators have called it the 'brotherhood of man.' Neither of these expressions is possible to use anywhere outside of heaven, for community of interest at once suggests to the mind a kind of happy condition where everybody wants the same thing and everybody gets it. This is [a] comparatively recent doctrine, but at least the liberty of the individual has been obtained, and we must face new theories.

To state it plainly, competition has been shown to be useful up to a certain point, but co-operation, which is the thing that we must strive for today, begins where competition leaves off. This was what the founders of the republic were groping for and it is precisely today along every possible walk of life.

Let us take some examples of this—for instance what we call today, conservation. We are taking merely a theory which began to develop in other countries many years ago. It was recognized in Germany for instance a hundred years ago that the trees on the land were necessary for the preservation of the water power and indeed for the general health and prosperity of the people. One hundred and fifty years ago in Germany the individual was not restricted from denuding his lands of the growing trees. Today he must cut only in a manner scientifically worked out, which is calculated to serve the ends of the community and not his ends.

They passed beyond the liberty of the individual to do as he pleased with his own property and found it was necessary to check this liberty for the benefit of the freedom of the whole people. So it is in New York State today. We are beginning to see that it is necessary for our health and happiness and the rights of individuals that lumber companies may not do as they please with the wooded growths in the Catskills and the Adirondacks.

There are, however, many persons who still think that individuals can do as they please with their own property even though it affects a community. The most striking example of what happens in such a case that I know of, was a picture shown me by Gifford Pinchot last week. It was a photograph of a walled city in northern China. Four or five hundred years ago this city had been the center of the populous and prosperous district, a district whose mountains and ridges were covered with magnificent trees, its streams flowing without interruption and its crops in the valleys prospering. It was known as one of the richest provinces in China, both as a lumber exporting center and as an agricultural community.

Today the picture shows the walled town, almost as it stood 500 years ago, but there is not a human being within the walls, and but few in the whole region. Rows upon rows of bare ridges and mountains stretch back from the city without a vestige of life. Everything is in a dilapidated condition, and this is all due to the liberty of the individual. This is what will happen in this very State if the individuals are allowed to do as they please with the natural resources to line their own pockets during their life. With them the motto is 'After us the deluge.' They do not care what happens after they are gone and even do not care what happens to their neighbors. . . .

There is, to my mind, no valid reason why the food supply of the nation should not be put on the most economical and at the same time the most productive basis by carrying out co-operation. If we call the method regulation, people hold up their hands in horror and say 'Unamerican,' or 'dangerous,' but if we call the same identical process co-operation these same old fogies will cry out 'well done.' It may seem absurd to call the rebating formerly done by railroads, and the great trusts so-called, minor issues, but after all rebating was discrimination and the doctrine of co-operation came with it. The same with trusts, they were and are run on the theory of monopoly, but co-operation puts monopoly out of date and we now understand that the mere size of a trust is not of necessity its evil. The trust is evil because it monopolizes for a few and as long as this keeps up it will be necessary for a community to change its features.

And here I come to the final point. How must the liberty of the community be obtained? It will not be obtained at once, whether the Democrats, Republicans or Socialists say so or not. It must be worked out by keeping ever in view the cause of the condition and we must also keep in view the other essential point: Law and order.[4]

ASSISTANT SECRETARY OF THE NAVY

FDR entered upon his new duties as Assistant Secretary of the Navy with characteristic gusto. He soon became involved in a wide range of domestic and foreign problems. One of his most memorable experiences was his inspection trip along the European battlefronts in 1918. While in France FDR kept an unpublished journal in which he recorded his impressions of the great and the nearly great. In his involvement with military matters he revealed much enthusiasm, as his entries indicate. Altogether, his war-time experiences greatly expanded his vision.

[LONDON, July 22, 1918]

Last night one of the famous Gray's Inn dinners—a really historic occasion—in honor of the War Ministers. Lord Curzon spoke—a defense of the War Cabinet, or rather a review of what England had done and is doing. Sir Robert Borden responded for Canada, General Smuts for South Africa, and, to my horror, the Italian Ambassador and I were called on without warning at the close to speak for the Allies . . .

I had a very good talk with Lloyd George . . . Lloyd George is just like his pictures, thick set, not very tall, rather a large head and rather long hair, but what impressed me more than anything else was his tremendous vitality. There is no question that the great majority of England is standing loyally behind him on the sole issue of winning the war . . . talked over the labor situation both here and at home. He said that, of course, the weakness of the British Government's position has all come

---

[4] F. D. Roosevelt from an address to the People's Forum at Troy, New York, March 3, 1912; from the Poughkeepsie, New York *News-Press*, March 5, 1912.

from the failure to adopt conscription at the outbreak of the war, and I suggested to him that in the same way we should have had vastly more trouble if we had not had the draft law as the final lever to insure continuation of work. I ventured to suggest that in my opinion the British Unions would obtain no sympathy from our Federation of Labor in any action involving a tie-up of war work. He seemed greatly pleased. . . .[5]

[July 28, 1918]

A very interesting day yesterday, came in from Cliveden in the morning, dressed and went to Buckingham Palace at 10:30 and had forty minutes all alone with the King. We drove to the "new front" of Buckingham Palace, which has been pasted on since I was here in 1905. I say "pasted" on because from almost any angle you see the other sides of Buckingham Palace, and the new façade is obviously an unsuccessful attempt to hide the earlier style. I was accompanied by Admiral Everett and Captain McCauley, and we passed through several corridors lined with paintings of naval actions that I would have given anything to stop and look at, thence up a half-flight to a charming little room with some very good Chinese lacquer ornaments, etc. I hope they were presents from the China Imperial family and not acquired as a result of the expedition of 1900. . . .

A gentleman in a frock coat soon conducted us up another half-flight to the King's study. The King has a nice smile and a very open, quick and cordial way of greeting one. He is not as short as I had expected, and I think his face is stronger than photographs make it appear. This is perhaps because his way of speaking is incisive. We talked for a while about American work in general and the Navy in particular. He seemed delighted that I had come over in a destroyer and said his one regret was that it had been impossible for him to do active naval service during the war. . . .

Then the subject switched to the Germans and he told me a lot about the atrocities in Belgium and northern France—many examples which had been proved true but which were too horrible to be placed even in the French official report or the report of Lord Bryce. Our troops had just reoccupied Château-Thierry and had found examples of wanton destruction of property by the Germans before they left, such as the smashing of pictures, breaking of furniture, etc. The King said he hoped that this at least would persuade the American people that the stories of outrageous destruction were true, and I agreed with him that there had been

[5] *Diary File*, Franklin D. Roosevelt Library, Hyde Park, N. Y.

a singular unwillingness in the United States to accept even the official reports of England and France.

I then remarked something about having been to school in Germany and having seen their preparation for the first stages of the war machine. The King said he went to school in Germany, too, for a year; then with a twinkle in his eye—"You know I have a number of relations in Germany, but I can tell you frankly that in all my life I have never seen a German gentleman."

The King said he had just had a nice letter from Uncle Ted. . . . We had just had news of Quentin's probable death, and the King expressed much sympathy. . . .

He was a delightfully easy person to talk to, and one got going so well that part of the time we were both talking at the same time. I understand that this type of interview is supposed to last only fifteen minutes, but it was nearly three-quarters of an hour before the King made a move. I said goodbye, and went back to the Chinese room, where I found McC. and the gentlemen-in-waiting looking at each other hopelessly. . . .[6]

POLIO

In contrast to the active and exuberant life that FDR led during World War I, his pace slackened greatly after August, 1921, when he was struck down with polio. Then the former athlete faced the most trying period of his personal life. Scores of letters from well-wishers and acquaintances poured in, many of which FDR answered with a cheerful optimism, perhaps sincere, perhaps contrived. An example is the note below to Walter Camp, famous Yale football coach, under whom FDR had done physical exercises in war-time Washington (1917-1918). Despite slow progress, three years later he was still optimistic and determined to recover. The communication describing his illness which he sent to a physician underscores his courage and hope which this crisis brought to the foreground, while reflecting as well his inclination for clinical detail.

WARM SPRINGS, GEORGIA
October 11, 1924

My dear Dr. Egleston:

Please excuse my delay in replying to your letter which has been forwarded to me down here in your neighboring state where I am spending a few weeks swimming and getting sunlight for my legs.

[6] *Ibid.*

I am very glad to tell you what I can in regard to my case and as I have talked it over with a great many doctors can, I think, give you a history of the case which would be equal to theirs.

First symptoms of the illness appeared in August, 1921, when I was thoroughly tired from overwork. I first had a chill in the evening which lasted practically all night. The following morning the muscles of the right knee appeared weak and by afternoon I was unable to support my weight on my right leg. That evening the left knee began to weaken also and by the following morning I was unable to stand up. This was accompanied by a continuing temperature of about 102 and I felt thoroughly achy all over. By the end of the third day practically all muscles from the chest down were involved. Above the chest the only symptom was a weakening of the two large thumb muscles making it impossible to write. There was no special pain along the spine and no rigidity of the neck.

For the following two weeks I had to be catheterized and there was slight, though not severe, difficulty in controlling the bowels. The fever lasted for only 6 or 7 days, but all the muscles from the hips down were extremely sensitive to the touch and I had to have the knees supported by pillows. This condition of extreme discomfort lasted about three weeks. I was then moved to a New York hospital and finally moved home in November, being able by that time to sit up in a wheel chair, but the leg muscles remained extremely sensitive and this sensitiveness disappeared gradually over a period of 6 months, the last remaining point being the calf muscles.

As to treatment—the mistake was made for the first 10 days of giving my feet and lower legs rather heavy massage. This was stopped by Dr. Lovett of Boston who was, without doubt, the greatest specialist on infantile paralysis. In January, 1922, 5 months after the attack he found that the muscles behind the knees had contracted and that there was a tendency to foot-drop in the right foot. These were corrected by the use of plaster casts during two weeks. In February, 1922, braces were fitted on each leg from the hips to the shoes, and I was able to stand up and learned gradually to walk with crutches. At the same time gentle exercises were begun, first every other day, then daily, exercising each muscle 10 times and seeking to avoid any undue strain by giving each muscle the correct movement with gravity. These exercises I did on a board placed on the bed.

The recovery of muscle paralysis began at this time, though for many months it seemed to make little progress. In the summer of 1922 I began swimming and found that this exercise seemed better adapted than any other because all weight was removed from the legs and I was able to move the legs in the water far better than I had expected. Since that time, i.e., for the last two years, I have as far as possible, in connection with my work and other duties, carried out practically the same treatment with the result that the muscles have increased in power to a remarkable extent and the improvement in the past 6 months has been even more rapid than at any previous time.

I still wear braces, of course, because the quadriceps are not yet strong enough to bear my weight. One year ago I was able to stand in fresh water without braces when the water was up to my chin. Six months ago I could stand in water up to the top of my shoulders and today can stand in water just level with my arm pits. This is a very simple method for me of determining how fast the quadriceps are coming back. Aside from these muscles the waist muscles on the right side are still weak and the outside muscles on the right leg have strengthened so much more than the inside muscles that they pull my right foot outward. I continue corrective exercises for all the muscles.

* * *

To sum up I would give you the following "Don'ts":

Don't use heavy massage but use light massage rubbing always towards the heart.

Don't let the patient over-exercise any muscle or get tired.

Don't let the patient feel cold, especially the legs, feet or any other part affected. Progress stops entirely when the legs or feet are cold.

Don't let the patient get too fat.

The following treatment is so far the best judging from my own experience and that of hundreds of other cases which I have studied:

1. Gentle exercise especially for the muscles which seem to be worst affected.

2. Gentle skin rubbing—not muscle kneading—bearing in mind that good circulation is a prime requisite.

3. Swimming in warm water—lots of it.

4. Sunlight—all the patient can get, especially direct sunlight on the affected parts. It would be ideal to lie in the sun all day with nothing on. This is difficult to accomplish but the nearest approach to it is a bathing suit.

5. Belief on the patient's part that the muscles are coming back and will eventually regain recovery of the affected parts. There are cases known in Norway where adults have taken the disease and not been able to walk until after a lapse of 10 or even 12 years.

I hope that your patient has not got a very severe case. They all differ, of course, in the degree in which the parts are affected. If braces are necessary there is a man in New York, whose name I will send you if you wish when I get back to New York, who makes remarkable light braces of duraluminum. My first braces of steel weighed 7 lbs. apiece—my new ones weigh only 4 lbs. apiece. Remember that braces are only for the convenience of the patient in getting around—a leg in a brace does not have a chance for muscle development. This must come through exercise when the brace is not on—such as swimming, etc.

I trust that your own daughter is wholly well again. . . .[7]

STATESMAN: COMMONWEALTH CLUB ADDRESS

Although FDR rarely dealt with abstract problems or with general theories, he did outline some of his fundamental beliefs about the nature of modern government in a memorable campaign address to the Commonwealth Club in San Francisco in September, 1932. In this speech FDR pointed particularly to problems created by industrialism in the twentieth century which necessitated a greater degree of government intervention than in previous years. The speech reflects a further development of ideas which he first outlined in his 1912 talk at Troy, New York (See above, p. 16).

In American political life, the new day, the day of the individual against the system, the day in which individualism was made the great watchword of American life.

The happiest of economic conditions made that day long and splendid. On the western frontier land was substantially free. No one who did not shirk the task of earning a living was entirely without opportunity to do so. Depressions could, and did, come and go; but they could not alter the fundamental fact that most of the people lived partly by selling their labor and partly by extracting their livelihood from the soil, so that starvation and dislocation were practically impossible.

At the very worst there was always the possibility of climbing into a covered wagon and moving West, where the untilled prairies afforded a haven for men to whom the East did not provide a place.

[7] From "A History of the Case in Franklin D. Roosevelt's Own Words," *The Journal of the South Carolina Medical Association* (January, 1946), pp. 1-2. (Copyright, 1946, by Mrs. William Egleston.)

So great were our natural resources that we could offer this relief not only to our own people but to the distressed of all the world. We could invite immigration from Europe and welcome it with open arms.

Traditionally, when a depression came a new section of land was opened in the West. And even our temporary misfortune served our manifest destiny.

It was in the middle of the nineteenth century that a new force was released and a new dream created. The force was what is called the industrial revolution, the advance of steam and machinery and the rise of the forerunners of the modern industrial plant.

The dream was the dream of an economic machine, able to raise the standard of living for everyone; to bring luxury within the reach of the humblest; to annihilate distance by steam power and later by electricity, and to release everyone from the drudgery of the heaviest manual toil.

It was to be expected that this would necessarily affect government. Heretofore, government had merely been called upon to produce conditions within which people could live happily, labor peacefully and rest secure. Now it was called upon to aid in the consummation of this new dream.

There was, however, a shadow over this dream. To be made real it required use of the talents of men of tremendous will and tremendous ambition, since by no other force could the problems of financing and engineering and new developments be brought to a consummation.

So manifest were the advantages of the machine age, however, that the United States fearlessly, cheerfully and, I think, rightly accepted the bitter with the sweet.

It was thought that no price was too high to pay for the advantages which we could draw from a finished industrial system.

The history of the last half century is accordingly in large measure a history of a group of financial titans, whose methods were not scrutinized with too much care and who were honored in proportion as they produced the results, irrespective of the means they used.

The financiers who pushed the railroads to the Pacific were always ruthless, often wasteful and frequently corrupt, but they did build railroads and we have them today.

It has been estimated that the American investor paid for the American railway system more than three times over in the process, but despite this fact the net advantage was to the United States.

As long as we had free land, as long as population was growing by leaps and bounds, as long as our industrial plants were insufficient to supply

our own needs, society chose to give the ambitious man free play and unlimited reward, provided only that he produced the economic plant so
much desired.

During this period of expansion there was equal opportunity for all,
and the business of government was not to interfere but to assist in the
development of industry.

This was done at the request of business men themselves. The tariff
was originally imposed for the purpose of "fostering our infant industry,"
a phrase I think the older among you will remember as a political issue
not so long ago.

The railroads were subsidized, sometimes by grants of money, oftener
by grants of land. Some of the most valuable oil lands in the United
States were granted to assist the financing of the railroad which pushed
through the Southwest.

A nascent merchant marine was assisted by grants of money or by mail
subsidies, so that our steam shipping might ply the seven seas.

Some of my friends tell me that they do not want the government in
business. With this I agree, but I wonder whether they realize the implications of the past.

For while it has been American doctrine that the government must not
go into business in competition with private enterprises, still it has been
traditional, particularly in Republican administrations, for business ur-
gently to ask the government to put at private disposal all kinds of government assistance.

The same man who tells you that he does not want to see the government interfere in business—and he means it and has plenty of good reasons for saying so—is the first to go to Washington and ask the government for a prohibitory tariff on his product.

When things get just bad enough—as they did two years ago—he will
go with equal speed to the United States Government and ask for a loan.
And the Reconstruction Finance Corporation is the outcome of it.

Each group has sought protection from the government for its own
special interests without realizing that the function of government must
be to favor no small group at the expense of its duty to protect the rights
of personal freedom and of private property of all its citizens.

In retrospect we can now see that the turn of the tide came with the
turn of the century. We were reaching our last frontier; there was no
more free land and our industrial combinations had become great uncon-
trolled and irresponsible units of power within the State.

Clear-sighted men saw with fear the danger that opportunity would no
longer be equal; that the growing corporation, like the feudal baron of

old, might threaten the economic freedom of individuals to earn a living. In that hour our antitrust laws were born.

The cry was raised against the great corporations. Theodore Roosevelt, the first great Republican Progressive, fought a Presidential campaign on the issue of "trust busting" and talked freely about malefactors of great wealth. If the government had a policy it was rather to turn the clock back, to destroy the large combinations and to return to the time when every man owned his individual small business.

This was impossible. Theodore Roosevelt, abandoning the idea of "trust busting," was forced to work out a difference between "good" and "bad" trusts.

The Supreme Court set forth the famous "rule of reason" by which it seems to have meant that a concentration of industrial power was permissible if the method by which it got its power, and the use it made of that power, was reasonable.

Woodrow Wilson, elected in 1912, saw the situation more clearly. Where Jefferson had feared the encroachment of political power on the lives of individuals, Wilson knew that the new power was financial. He saw, in the highly centralized economic system, the despot of the twentieth century, on whom great masses of individuals relied for their safety and their livelihood, and whose irresponsibility and greed (if it were not controlled) would reduce them to starvation and penury.

The concentration of financial power had not proceeded so far in 1912 as it has today, but it had grown far enough for Mr. Wilson to realize fully its implications. . . .

A glance at the situation today only too clearly indicates that equality of opportunity as we have known it no longer exists. Our industrial plant is built. The problem just now is whether, under existing conditions, it is not overbuilt.

Our last frontier has long since been reached, and there is practically no more free land. More than half of our people do not live on the farms or on lands and cannot derive a living by cultivating their own property.

There is no safety valve in the form of a Western prairie to which those thrown out of work by the Eastern economic machines can go for a new start. We are not able to invite the immigration from Europe to share our endless plenty. We are now providing a drab living for our own people.

Our system of constantly rising tariffs has at last reacted against us to the point of closing our Canadian frontier on the north, our European markets on the east, many of our Latin-American markets to the south and a goodly proportion of our Pacific markets on the west through the retaliatory tariffs of those countries.

It has forced many of our great industrial institutions, who exported their surplus production to such countries, to establish plants in such countries, within the tariff walls.

This has resulted in the reduction of the operation of their American plants and opportunity for employment.

Just as freedom to farm has ceased, so also the opportunity in business has narrowed. It still is true that men can start small enterprises, trusting to native shrewdness and ability to keep abreast of competitors; but area after area has been pre-empted altogether by the great corporations, and even in the fields which still have no great concerns the small man starts under a handicap.

The unfeeling statistics of the past three decades show that the independent business man is running a losing race. Perhaps he is forced to the wall; perhaps he cannot command credit; perhaps he is "squeezed out," in Mr. Wilson's words, by highly organized corporate competitors, as your corner grocery man can tell you.

Recently a careful study was made of the concentration of business in the United States.

It showed that our economic life was dominated by some 600-odd corporations who controlled two-thirds of American industry. Ten million small business men divided the other third.

More striking still, it appeared that if the process of concentration goes on at the same rate, at the end of another century we shall have all American industry controlled by a dozen corporations and run by perhaps a hundred men.

Put plainly, we are steering a steady course toward economic oligarchy, if we are not there already.

Clearly, all this calls for a re-appraisal of values.

A mere builder of more industrial plants, a creator of more railroad systems, an organizer of more corporations, is as likely to be a danger as a help.

The day of the great promoter or the financial titan, to whom we granted anything if only he would build or develop, is over. Our task now is not discovery or exploitation of natural resources or necessarily producing more goods.

＊　　＊　　＊

The day of enlightened administration has come.

Just as in older times the central government was first a haven of refuge and then a threat, so now in a closer economic system the central and ambitious financial unit is no longer a servant of national desire but a danger. I would draw the parallel one step further. We did not think because national government had become a threat in the eighteenth century that therefore we should abandon the principle of national government.

Nor today should be abandon the principle of strong economic units called corporations merely because their power is susceptible of easy abuse.

In other times we dealt with the problem of an unduly ambitious central government by modifying it gradually into a constitutional democratic government. So today we are modifying and controlling our economic units.

As I see it, the task of government in its relation to business is to assist the development of an economic declaration of rights, an economic constitutional order. This is the common task of statesman and business man. It is the minimum requirement of a more permanently safe order of things. . . .

Every man has a right to life, and this means that he has also a right to make a comfortable living. He may by sloth or crime decline to exercise that right, but it may not be denied him.

We have no actual famine or dearth; our industrial and agricultural mechanism can produce enough and to spare.

Our government formal and informal, political and economic, owes to every one an avenue to possess himself of a portion of that plenty sufficient for his needs through his own work.

Every man has a right to his own property, which means a right to be assured, to the fullest extent attainable, in the safety of his savings. By no other means can men carry the burdens of those parts of life which in the nature of things afford no chance of labor—childhood, sickness, old age.

In all thought of property, this right is paramount; all other property rights must yield to it.

If, in accord with this principle, we must restrict the operations of the speculator, the manipulator, even the financier, I believe we must accept the restriction as needful not to hamper individualism but to protect it. . . .

The government should assume the function of economic regulation only as a last resort, to be tried only when private initiative, inspired by high responsibility, with such assistance and balance as government can give, has finally failed.

As yet there has been no final failure, because there has been no attempt; and I decline to assume that this nation is unable to meet the situation.

The final term of the high contract was for liberty and the pursuit of happiness.

We have learned a great deal of both in the past century. We know that individual liberty and individual happiness mean nothing unless both are ordered in the sense that one man's meat is not another man's poison.

We know that the old "rights of personal competency"—the right to read, to think, to speak, to choose and live a mode of life,—must be respected at all hazards.

We know that liberty to do anything which deprives others of those elemental rights is outside the protection of any compact, and that government in this regard is the maintenance of a balance within which every individual may have a place if he will take it, in which every individual may find safety if he wishes it, in which every individual may attain such power as his ability permits, consistent with his assuming the accompanying responsibility. . . .

Faith in America, faith in our tradition of personal responsibility, faith in our institutions, faith in ourselves demands that we recognize the new terms of the old social contact.

We shall fulfill them, as we fulfilled the obligation of the apparent utopia which Jefferson imagined for us in 1776 and which Jefferson, Roosevelt and Wilson sought to bring to realization.

We must do so, lest a rising tide of misery, engendered by our common failure, engulf us all.

But failure is not an American habit, and in the strength of great hope we must all shoulder our common load.[8]

[8] *The New York Times,* September 24, 1932.

2

The Presidency

Ironically, FDR's infectious optimism was perhaps never more manifest than in the lowest depths of the depression. In his first Inaugural Address—destined to be one of his most memorable speeches—FDR expressed his positive approach to life, while frankly stating the difficulties that face the nation. The tone of this call to action aroused millions of Americans, and was perhaps more significant than the particular promises which he made. The following portion of the speech evokes the atmosphere of hope and despair in which it was delivered.

THE NEW PRESIDENT: THE FIRST INAUGURAL

I am certain that my fellow Americans expect that on my induction into the Presidency I will address them with a candor and a decision which the present situation of our Nation impels. This is preeminently the time to speak the truth, the whole truth, frankly and boldly. Nor need we shrink from honestly facing conditions in our country today. This great Nation will endure as it has endured, will revive and will prosper. So, first of all, let me assert my firm belief that the only thing we have to fear is fear itself—nameless, unreasoning, unjustified terror which paralyzes needed efforts to convert retreat into advance. In every dark hour of our national life a leadership of frankness and vigor has met with that understanding and support of the people themselves which is essential to victory. I am convinced that you will again give that support to leadership in these critical days.

In such a spirit on my part and on yours we face our common difficulties. They concern, thank God, only material things. Values have shrunken to fantastic levels; taxes have risen; our ability to pay has fallen; government of all kinds is faced by serious curtailment of income; the means of exchange are frozen in the currents of trade; the withered leaves of industrial enterprise lie on every side; farmers find no markets for their produce; the savings of many years in thousands of families are gone.

More important, a host of unemployed citizens face the grim problem

31

of existence, and an equally great number toil with little return. Only a foolish optimist can deny the dark realities of the moment.

Yet our distress comes from no failure of substance. We are stricken by no plague of locusts. Compared with the perils which our forefathers conquered because they believed and were not afraid, we have still much to be thankful for. Nature still offers her bounty and human efforts have multiplied it. Plenty is at our doorstep, but a generous use of it languishes in the very sight of the supply. Primarily this is because rulers of the exchange of mankind's goods have failed through their own stubbornness and their own incompetence, have admitted their failure, and have abdicated. Practices of the unscrupulous money changers stand indicted in the court of public opinion, rejected by the hearts and minds of men.

True they have tried, but their efforts have been cast in the pattern of an outworn tradition. Faced by failure of credit they have proposed only the lending of more money. Stripped of the lure of profit by which to induce our people to follow their false leadership, they have resorted to exhortations, pleading tearfully for restored confidence. They know only the rules of a generation of self-seekers. They have no vision, and when there is no vision the people perish.

The money changers have fled from their high seats in the temple of our civilization. We may now restore that temple to the ancient truths. The measure of the restoration lies in the extent to which we apply social values more noble than mere monetary profit.

Happiness lies not in the mere possession of money; it lies in the joy of achievement, in the thrill of creative effort. The joy and moral stimulation of work no longer must be forgotten in the mad chase of evanescent profits. These dark days will be worth all they cost us if they teach us that our true destiny is not to be ministered unto but to minister to ourselves and to our fellow men.

Recognition of the falsity of material wealth as the standard of success goes hand in hand with the abandonment of the false belief that public office and high political position are to be valued only by the standards of pride of place and personal profit; and there must be an end to a conduct in banking and in business which too often has given to a sacred trust the likeness of callous and selfish wrongdoing. Small wonder that confidence languishes, for it thrives only on honesty, on honor, on the sacredness of obligations, on faithful protection, on unselfish performance; without them it cannot live.

Restoration calls, however, not for changes in ethics alone. This Nation asks for action, and action now.

Our greatest primary task is to put people to work. This is no unsolvable problem if we face it wisely and courageously. It can be accomplished in part by direct recruiting by the Government itself, treating the task as we would treat the emergency of a war, but at the same time, through this employment, accomplishing greatly needed projects to stimulate and reorganize the use of our natural resources.

Hand in hand with this we must frankly recognize the overbalance of population in our industrial centers and, by engaging on a national scale in a redistribution, endeavor to provide a better use of the land for those best fitted for the land. The task can be helped by definite efforts to raise the values of agricultural products and with this the power to purchase the output of our cities. It can be helped by preventing realistically the tragedy of the growing loss through foreclosure of our small homes and our farms. It can be helped by insistence that the Federal, State, and local governments act forthwith on the demand that their cost be drastically reduced. It can be helped by the unifying of relief activities which today are often scattered, uneconomical, and unequal. It can be helped by national planning for and supervision of all forms of transportation and of communications and other utilities which have a definitely public character. There are many ways in which it can be helped, but it can never be helped merely by talking about it. We must act and act quickly.

Finally, in our progress toward a resumption of work we require two safeguards against a return of the evils of the old order: there must be a strict supervision of all banking and credits and investments, so that there will be an end to speculation with other people's money; and there must be provision for an adequate but sound currency.

These are the lines of attack. I shall presently urge upon a new Congress, in special session, detailed measures for their fulfillment, and I shall seek the immediate assistance of the several States.

Through this program of action we address ourselves to putting our own national house in order and making income balance outgo. Our international trade relations, though vastly important, are in point of time and necessity secondary to the establishment of a sound national economy. I favor as a practical policy the putting of first things first. I shall spare no effort to restore world trade by international economic readjustment, but the emergency at home cannot wait on that accomplishment.

The basic thought that guides these specific means of national recovery is not narrowly nationalistic. It is the insistence, as a first consideration, upon the interdependence of the various elements in and parts of the United States—a recognition of the old and permanently important manifestation of the American spirit of the pioneer. It is the way to recovery. It is the immediate way. It is the strongest assurance that the recovery will endure.

In the field of world policy I would dedicate this Nation to the policy of the good neighbor—the neighbor who resolutely respects himself and, because he does so, respects the rights of others—the neighbor who respects his obligations and respects the sanctity of his agreements in and with a world of neighbors.

If I read the temper of our people correctly, we now realize as we have never realized before our interdependence on each other; that we cannot merely take but we must give as well; that if we are to go forward, we must move as a trained and loyal army willing to sacrifice for the good of a common discipline, because without such discipline no progress is made, no leadership becomes effective. We are, I know, ready and willing to submit our lives and property to such discipline, because it makes possible a leadership which aims at a larger good. This I propose to offer, pledging that the larger purposes will bind upon us all as a sacred obligation with a unity of duty hitherto evoked only in time of armed strife.

With this pledge taken, I assume unhesitatingly the leadership of this great army of our people dedicated to a disciplined attack upon our common problems. . . .[1]

THE GREAT EXPERIMENTER:
FIRESIDE CHAT AMIDST THE FIRST HUNDRED DAYS

Despite the frenzied action of his first three months in office, FDR developed then one of his most potent and effective means of communicating with the American people—the Fireside Chat. Endowed with a magnificent radio voice, FDR used these periodic radio addresses to explain his policies to millions of listeners in clear and simple language. One of the most significant Chats came in the course of the First Hundred Days while Congress and the White House were preparing a host of complicated measures which were the foundations of the New Deal's crisis program. The President therefore sought to make his Administration's intentions clear. The excerpts from his speech below evoke a little, perhaps, of that sense of intimacy which FDR was able to achieve with people gathered about their radio sets in living rooms across the land.

On a Sunday night a week after my Inauguration I used the radio to tell you about the banking crisis and the measures we were taking to

[1] *The New York Times,* March 5, 1933.

meet it. I think that in that way I made clear to the country various facts that might otherwise have been misunderstood and in general provided a means of understanding which did much to restore confidence.

Tonight, eight weeks later, I come for the second time to give you my report; in the same spirit and by the same means to tell you about what we have been doing and what we are planning to do.

Two months ago we were facing serious problems. The country was dying by inches. It was dying because trade and commerce had declined to dangerously low levels; prices for basic commodities were such as to destroy the value of the assets of national institutions such as banks, savings banks, insurance companies, and others. These institutions, because of their great needs, were foreclosing mortgages, calling loans, refusing credit. Thus there was actually in process of destruction the property of millions of people who had borrowed money on that property in terms of dollars which had had an entirely different value from the level of March, 1933. That situation in that crisis did not call for any complicated consideration of economic panaceas or fancy plans. We were faced by a condition and not a theory.

There were just two alternatives: The first was to allow the foreclosures to continue, credit to be withheld and money to go into hiding, thus forcing liquidation and bankruptcy of banks, railroads and insurance companies and a recapitalizing of all business and all property on a lower level. This alternative meant a continuation of what is loosely called "deflation," the net result of which would have been extraordinary hardships on all property owners and, incidentally, extraordinary hardships on all persons working for wages through an increase in unemployment and a further reduction of the wage scale.

It is easy to see that the result of this course would have not only economic effects of a very serious nature, but social results that might bring incalculable harm. Even before I was inaugurated I came to the conclusion that such a policy was too much to ask the American people to bear. It involved not only a further loss of homes, farms, savings and wages, but also a loss of spiritual values—the loss of that sense of security for the present and the future so necessary to the peace and contentment of the individual and of his family. When you destroy these things you will find it difficult to establish confidence of any sort in the future. It was clear that mere appeals from Washington for confidence and the mere lending of more money to shaky institutions could not stop this downward course. A prompt program applied as quickly as possible seemed to me not only justified but imperative to our national security. The Congress, and when I say Congress I mean the members of both political parties, fully understood this and gave me generous and intelligent support. The members of Congress realized that the methods of normal times had to be replaced in the emergency by measures which were suited to the serious and pressing requirements of the moment. There was no actual surrender of power, Congress still retained its constitutional authority, and no one has the slightest desire to change the balance of these powers. The function of Congress is to decide what has to be done and to select the appropriate agency to carry out its will. To this policy it has strictly adhered. The only thing that has been happening has been to designate the President as the agency to carry out certain of the purposes of the Congress. This was constitutional and in keeping with the past American tradition.

The legislation which has been passed or is in the process of enactment can properly be considered as part of a well-grounded plan.

First, we are giving opportunity of employment to one-quarter of a million of the unemployed, especially the young men who have dependents, to go into the forestry and flood-prevention work. This is a big task because it means feeding, clothing and caring for nearly twice as many men as we have in the regular army itself. In creating this civilian conservation corps we are killing two birds with one stone. We are clearly enhancing the value of our natural resources, and we are relieving an appreciable amount of actual distress. This great group of men has entered upon its work on a purely voluntary basis; no military training is involved and we are conserving not only our natural resources, but our human resources. One of the great values to this work is the fact that it is direct and requires the intervention of very little machinery.

Second, I have requested the Congress and have secured action upon a proposal to put the great properties owned by our Government at Muscle Shoals to work after long years of wasteful inaction, and with this a broad plan for the improvement of a vast area in the Tennessee Valley. It will add to the comfort and happiness of hundreds of thousands of people and the incident benefits will reach the entire Nation.

Next, the Congress is about to pass legislation that will greatly ease the mortgage distress among the farmers and the home owners of the Nation, by providing for the easing of the burden of debt now bearing so heavily upon millions of our people.

Our next step in seeking immediate relief is a grant of half a billion dollars to help the States, counties and municipalities in their duty to care for those who need direct and immediate relief.

The Congress also passed legislation authorizing the sale of beer in such States as desired it. This has already resulted in considerable re-employment and incidentally has provided much-needed tax revenue.

We are planning to ask the Congress for legislation to enable the Government to undertake public works, thus stimulating directly and indirectly the employment of many others in well-considered projects.

Further legislation has been taken up which goes much more fundamentally into our economic problems. The Farm Relief Bill seeks by the use of several methods, alone or together, to bring about an increased return to farmers for their major farm products, seeking at the same time to prevent in the days to come disastrous overproduction which so often in the past has kept farm commodity prices far below a reasonable return. This measure provides wide powers for emergencies. The extent of its use will depend entirely upon what the future has in store.

Well-considered and conservative measures will likewise be proposed which will attempt to give to the industrial workers of the country a more fair wage return, prevent cut-throat competition and unduly long hours for labor, and at the same time encourage each industry to prevent overproduction.

Our Railroad Bill falls into the same class because it seeks to provide and make certain definite planning by the railroads themselves, with the assistance of the Government, to eliminate the duplication and waste that is now resulting in railroad receiverships and continuing operating deficits.

I am certain that the people of this country understand and approve the broad purposes behind these new governmental policies relating to agriculture and industry and transportation. We found ourselves faced with more agricultural products than we could possibly consume ourselves and with surpluses which other Nations did not have the cash to buy from us except at prices ruinously low. We found our factories able to turn out more goods than we could possibly consume, and at the same time we were faced with a falling export demand. We found ourselves with more facilities to transport goods and crops than there were goods and crops to be transported. All of this has been caused in large part by a complex lack of planning and a complete failure to understand the danger signals that have been flying ever since the close of the World War. The people of this country have been erroneously encouraged to believe that they could keep on increasing the output of farm and factory indefinitely and that some magician would find ways and means for that increased output to be consumed with reasonable profit to the producer.

Today we have reason to believe that things are a little better than they were two months ago. Industry has picked up, railroads are carrying more freight, farm prices are better, but I am not going to indulge in issuing proclamations of over-enthusiastic assurance. We cannot ballyhoo ourselves back to prosperity. I am going to be honest at all times with the people of the country. I do not want the people of this country to take the foolish course of letting this improvement come back on another speculative wave. I do not want the people to believe that because of unjustified optimism we can resume the ruinous practice of increasing our crop output and our factory output in the hope that a kind Providence will find buyers at high prices. Such a course may bring us immediate and false prosperity but it will be the kind of prosperity that will lead us into another tailspin.

It is wholly wrong to call the measures that we have taken Government control of farming, industry, and transportation. It is rather a partnership between Government and farming and industry and transportation, not partnership in profits, for the profits still go to the citizens, but rather a partnership in planning, and a partnership to see that the plans are carried out.

* * *

We are working toward a definite goal, which is to prevent the return of conditions which came very close to destroying what we call modern civilization. The actual accomplishment of our purpose cannot be attained in a day. Our policies are wholly within purposes for which our American Constitutional Government was established 150 years ago.

I know that the people of this country will understand this and will also understand the spirit in which we are undertaking this policy. I do not deny that we may make mistakes of procedure as we carry out the policy. I have no expectation of making a hit every time I come to bat. What I seek is the highest possible batting average, not only for myself but for the team. Theodore Roosevelt once said to me: "If I can be right 75 percent of the time I shall come up to the fullest measure of my hopes."

* * *

Hand in hand with the domestic situation which, of course, is our first concern is the world situation, and I want to emphasize to you that the domestic situation is inevitably and deeply tied in with the conditions in all of the other Nations of the world. In other words, we can get, in all probability, a fair measure of prosperity to return in the United States, but it will not be permanent unless we get a return to prosperity all over the world.

In the conferences which we have held and are holding with the leaders of other Nations, we are seeking four great objectives: first, a general reduction of armaments and through this the removal of the fear of invasion and armed attack, and, at the same time, a reduction in armament costs, in order to help in the balancing of Government budgets and the reduction of taxation; second, a cutting down of the trade barriers, in order to restart the flow of exchange of crops and goods between Nations; third, the setting up of a stabilization of currencies, in order that trade can make contracts ahead; fourth, the reestablishment of friendly relations and greater confidence between all Nations.

Our foreign visitors these past three weeks have responded to these purposes in a very helpful way. All of the Nations have suffered alike in this great depression. They have all reached the conclusion that each can best be helped by the common action of all. It is in this spirit that our visitors have met with us and discussed our common problems. The international conference that lies before us must succeed. The future of the world demands it and we have each of us pledged ourselves to the best joint efforts to this end.

To you, the people of this country, all of us, the members of the Congress and the members of this Administration, owe a profound debt of gratitude. Throughout the depression you have been patient. You have granted us wide powers; you have encouraged us with a widespread approval of our purposes. Every ounce of strength and every resource at our command we have devoted to the end of justifying your confidence. We are encouraged to believe that a wise and sensible beginning has been made. In the present spirit of mutual confidence and mutual encouragement we go forward.[2]

BUSINESS: THE NRA

When the National Recovery Administration celebrated its first anniversary, FDR took the occasion to review his Administration's attitude towards business. In his extemporaneous remarks, excerpted below, FDR stressed his goal of maintaining, not subverting, American democratic institutions, for he was being accused of tendencies towards either Fascism or Communism. His strong emphasis on the need for cooperation between government and business was typical of the First New Deal attitude.

Eight and a half months ago when I signed the bill of the Congress creating the National Industrial Recovery Commission, I said this: "Must

[2] *The New York Times,* May 8, 1933.

we go on in many groping, disorganized, separate units to defeat or shall we move as one great team to victory?"

That team is before me this morning, four or five thousand strong, leaders of six hundred or more organized industries representing, as measured by employment, more than 90 percent of the industrial field which is covered by the N.R.A. Naturally I am deeply gratified that the faith which I expressed last June is so well justified in March.

I do not undertake today to present either a broad review of all the manifold causes which led up to the distressful situation from which the Nation is emerging or a recapitulation of the events, the measures and the results of this past year. You are here as the direct representatives of only one element in our complex modern life, but at the same time because of the fine spirit you have shown I can congratulate you on an approach to your own problems which shows an understanding of the many other problems which criss-cross and dovetail into each other to make up the broad objective of the American people.

It is sufficient for me to point out once more that the difficult and dangerous situation into which the United States had got itself was due to the general attitude, "Every man for himself; the devil take the hindmost." Individuals were seeking quick riches at the expense of other individuals. Geographical sections were seeking economic preference for themselves to the disadvantage of other sections. Cities were recklessly offering inducements to manufacturing plants to move away from other cities. Within given industries unfair competition went on unheeded or resulted in vast consolidations whose securities were peddled to the public at dishonest prices. There was little consideration for the social point of view, and no planning whatsoever to avoid the pitfalls of overproduction or of selling methods which foisted articles on a gullible public, which the family budget could not afford.

That is a strong picture but you and I, in the bottom of our hearts, know that it is a true picture. Most of us participated in the making of that picture. We did know as much then as we know now and because our eyes have been opened it is possible that future history will call that crazy decade of 1919 to 1929 one of the greatest blessings that ever came to the American people.

It was because the situation in March, 1933, was so serious all along the line that remedies had to be applied to every phase of the illness. The objective was, as you know, to apply these remedies in the American way and not to copy those which are being tried in other countries which do not live under the same form of democratic government as ours. I am always a little amused and perhaps at times a little saddened—and I think the American people feel the same way—by those few writers and speakers who proclaim tearfully either that we are now committed to Communism and collectivism or that we have adopted Fascism and a dictatorship. The real truth of the matter is that for a number of years in our country the machinery of democracy had failed to function. Through inertia on the part of leaders and on the part of the people themselves the operations of government had fallen into the hands of special groups, some of them vociferously led by people who undertook to obtain special advantages for special classes and others led by a handful of individuals who believed in their superhuman ability to retain in their own hands the entire business and financial control over the economic and social structure of the Nation.

The fine response given by the overwhelming majority of the component parts of industry as represented here today proves to me that you have the same understanding of our broad purpose as is held by the average of the workers of the United States—and that word "workers" means almost all of the American people. You have shown sincere desire for real cooperation; you have shown prompt response to the governmental request for national unity. For this support I give you my thanks.

The National Industrial Recovery Act was drawn with the greatest good of the greatest number in mind. Its aim was to increase the buying power of wage earners and farmers so that industry, labor and the public might benefit through building up the market for farm and factory goods. Employer, wage earner and consumer groups are all represented on its boards with the Government. All three groups with the Government must have the interests of all the people as their main responsibility.

What we seek is balance in our economic system—balance between agriculture and industry, and balance between the wage earner, the employer and the consumer. We seek also balance that our internal markets be kept rich and large, and that our trade with other Nations be increased on both sides of the ledger.

You and I are now conducting a great test to find out how the business leaders in all groups of industry can develop capacity to operate for the general welfare. Personally I am convinced that with your help the test is succeeding.

The very conception of N.R.A. follows the democratic procedure of our Government itself. Its theory of self-regulation follows the American method rather than any of the experiments being tried in other Nations. The very fact that you have been in Washington to criticize and to discuss the way N.R.A. is working out is sufficient proof of this point.

There are some people, of course, who do not think things through;

as, for example, the man who complained in one of yesterday morning's papers that criticism was held to be unpatriotic. Let me put the case so clearly that even his type will understand. If we admit that the Government has a specific problem to solve and undertakes to do it in a specific way, the critic is unpatriotic who contents himself with loudly proclaiming that that way, that method is no good; that it will not work; that it is wrong to do this. This critic contributes nothing; he is not constructive; he is unpatriotic because he attempts to destroy without even suggesting a way to build.

On the other hand, the critic is patriotic whether he be a business man, a worker, a farmer or a politician if he says, "I do not like the methods you are using to solve the problem; I believe it would be far better if we were to use the following alternate method," and if he thereupon outlines a helpful proposal for the benefit of his neighbor and his Government.

In this great evolution through which we are passing, the average American is doing splendid service by coming back at the captious critic and saying to him, "Well, old man, and what do *you* suggest?" One thing is very certain—we are not going back either to the old conditions or to the old methods.[3]

UNEMPLOYMENT

Perhaps the most nagging problem of the New Deal was unemployment. Until World War II FDR was never able to find effective remedies for joblessness. Yet he did not give up his hope that one day this blight could be eliminated from the American economy. He revealed this view in his second Fireside Chat of 1934 which is excerpted below.

Closely allied to the N.R.A. is the program of public works provided for in the same Act and designed to put more men back to work, both directly on the public works themselves, and indirectly in the industries supplying the materials for these public works. To those who say that our expenditures for public works and other means for recovery are a waste that we cannot afford, I answer that no country, however rich, can afford the waste of its human resources. Demoralization caused by vast unemployment is our greatest extravagance. Morally, it is the greatest menace to our social order. Some people try to tell me that we must make up our minds that for the future we shall permanently have millions of

[3] *The New York Times,* March 6, 1934.

unemployed just as other countries have had them for over a decade. What may be necessary for those countries is not my responsibility to determine. But as for this country, I stand or fall by my refusal to accept as a necessary condition of our future a permanent army of unemployed. On the contrary, we must make it a national principle that we will not tolerate a large army of unemployed and that we will arrange our national economy to end our present unemployment as soon as we can and then to take wise measures against its return. I do not want to think that it is the destiny of any American to remain permanently on relief rolls.[4]

REGIONAL DEVELOPMENT: THE TVA

FDR effectively combined his love for the outdoors with his zeal for conservation and reform. All of these motives were reflected in his enthusiastic espousal of the Tennessee Valley Authority, a multipurpose power authority in Alabama and a seven-state area in the South. After a visit to the TVA's facilities in 1934, FDR explained his goals for the project to reporters. Excerpts from that press conference appear below.

Q. Mr. President, is there anything you can tell us on the record concerning the visit of your various power officials here today?

THE PRESIDENT: They are members of a committee, I could not tell you the name of it, that has on it somebody from the Federal Trade Commission, somebody from T.V.A., somebody from Interior and one or two from the Power Commission. They have been working—I think the whole thing came out last spring—on a general survey of the power situation, and they are going to talk with me about that tonight.

Q. Is that your National Resources Committee?

THE PRESIDENT: No, it is separate from that. It relates only to power.

MR. TUGWELL: Manly can tell them about it. I have forgotten the name of the committee too.

THE PRESIDENT: It is one of the inter-departmental committees to report on the general situation.

Q. With recommendations for legislation?

THE PRESIDENT: Yes, and policy.

Q. Still on the record, does that visit here mean that you have in mind any new moves of a concrete nature in the immediate future in connection with what you were telling us the other day?

[4] *The New York Times*, October 1, 1934.

THE PRESIDENT: This has nothing to do with the trip or T.V.A. or anything like that, except in so far as it relates to general power policy. . . .

Q. I feel I am doing a lot of talking here, but the other day you spoke
of power and there are a lot of interpretations on it. Purely . . .

THE PRESIDENT: Oh, the interpretations are all pure. (*Laughter*)

Q. Do you mind telling us what your ideas are regarding private power
companies?

THE PRESIDENT: All right, I shall give you something on that, but this
has to be off the record because I don't want to be in the position of
interpreting what I said. (*Laughter*)

It is a perfectly simple thing. Two years ago, in this room, you were
here, Fred . . .

MR. STORM: I was here.

THE PRESIDENT: We spent an hour and a half. I think it was in January,
1933, and we had been down with Norris to see the Wilson Dam.
And I had said up there publicly that we were going ahead with the
development of Muscle Shoals. That is all I said at that time publicly.
We came down here and we had this talk in which I outlined what
developed into T.V.A. . . .

I can put it this way: Power is really a secondary matter. What we
are doing there is taking a watershed with about three and a half
million people in it, almost all of them rural, and we are trying to
make a different type of citizen out of them from what they would
be under their present conditions. Now, that applies not only to the
mountaineers—we all know about them—but it applies to the people
around Muscle Shoals. Do you remember that drive over to Wheeler
Dam the other day? You went through a county of Alabama where
the standards of education are lower than almost any other county in
the United States, and yet that is within twenty miles of the Muscle
Shoals Dam. They have never had a chance. All you had to do was to
look at the houses in which they lived. Heavens, this section around
here is 1,000 percent compared with that section we went through.
The homes through here are infinitely better.

So T.V.A. is primarily intended to change and to improve the
standards of living of the people of that valley. Power is, as I said,
a secondary consideration. Of course it is an important one because,
if you can get cheap power to those people, you hasten the process of
raising the standard of living.

The T.V.A. has been going ahead with power, yes, but it has been
going ahead with probably a great many other things besides power

and dam building. For instance, take fertilizer. You talk about a "yard-stick of power."

Dr. H. A. Morgan is running the fertilizer end of it and at Muscle Shoals he is turning out, not a nitrate—the plant was originally built for a nitrate plant—but he is turning out a phosphate. He is conducting a very fine experiment with phosphate of lime. They believe that for this whole area around here, and that would include this kind of soil around here, phosphate of lime is the best thing you can put on land in addition to being the cheapest.

Now at once, the fertilizer companies, the National Fertilizer Association that gets out figures (*laughter*), say, "Are you going into the fertilizer business?" The answer is a very simple one. The plant is primarily an experimental plant. That is the primary purpose. Therefore, they are going to take this year a thousand acres of Government land, worn-out land typical of the locality, and they are going to use this phosphate of lime on these thousand acres and show what can be done with the land. They are going to give a definite demonstration. They will compare it with the other fertilizers, putting them in parallel strips, and they will see which works out best and at the lowest cost. Having the large plant, they will be able to figure out what is a fair price for the best type of fertilizer.

Having done that and having figured out the fair price, it becomes a process of education. If the farmers all through that area can be taught that that type of fertilizer at x number of dollars a ton is the best thing for them to use, then it is up to the National Fertilizer Association and its affiliated companies to meet that price. Now, that is the real answer, and we hope that they will meet that price, adding to the cost of manufacture a reasonable profit. We shall know what the cost of manufacture is, and it is very easy to say what a reasonable profit is. Now, if those gentlemen fail to avail themselves of this magnificent opportunity to conduct a sound business and make a profit, well, it is just too bad. Then somebody will get up in Congress and say, "These fellows are not meeting their opportunities and the farmers will have to have the fertilizer and of course we shall have to provide it." But I, for one, hope that that day will never come. Now, that is not holding a big stick over them at all. It is saying to them, "Here is your opportunity. We go down on our knees to you, asking you to take it."

Q. Just a little guiding light.

THE PRESIDENT: In other words, what we are trying to do is something constructive to enable business . . .

MRS. ROOSEVELT: An intimation. (*Laughter*)

THE PRESIDENT: No, it is not even an intimation. No, it is a generous offer. Now, coming down to power. You take the example of Corinth we went through the other day. In Corinth, without Government assistance—they did it themselves—they had a county electric-power association and they used to buy their juice from the Mississippi Power Company. Because they were on a through line to Tupelo, the T.V.A. came along and stepped in as a middleman, and still bought the power from the Mississippi Power Company at a lower cost per kilowatt on the agreement with the Mississippi Power Company that it would take more juice. The result was that the Mississippi Power Company gets the same gross profit as it was getting before, but it is selling more power. Then the T.V.A., merely acting as middleman without any profit to itself, turns around and sells it to the county electric-power association. That part of it does not change the existing situation at all. The Mississippi Power Company merely gave a lower rate to the Alcorn County people, but it did it via the T.V.A., instead of direct. It was merely a bookkeeping matter. It does not cost the T.V.A. anything, and it does not receive anything.[5]

SOCIAL SECURITY

Prodded by reformers such as Francis Townsend, and consciously apprehensive over the approaching national elections, FDR embarked on social reforms for which he had shown some reluctance in the early days of the New Deal. Perhaps the most important of these measures was the Social Security Act. Always a pragmatist, FDR viewed it not only as a necessary reform, but also as a means to ameliorate the depression. His statement upon signing the act, which follows, summarizes these views.

Today a hope of many years' standing is in large part fulfilled. The civilization of the past hundred years, with its startling industrial changes, has tended more and more to make life insecure. Young people have come to wonder what would be their lot when they came to old age. The man with a job has wondered how long the job would last.

[5] *The One Hundred and Sixtieth Press Conference*, at Warm Springs, Georgia, November 23, 1934; from the Press Conference File, Franklin D. Roosevelt Library, Hyde Park, N. Y.

This social security measure gives at least some protection to thirty millions of our citizens who will reap direct benefits through unemployment compensation, through old-age pensions and through increased services for the protection of children and the prevention of ill health.

We can never insure one hundred percent of the population against one hundred percent of the hazards and vicissitudes of life, but we have tried to frame a law which will give some measure of protection to the average citizen and to his family against the loss of a job and against poverty-ridden old age.

This law, too, represents a cornerstone in a structure which is being built but is by no means complete. It is a structure intended to lessen the force of possible future depressions. It will act as a protection to future Administrations against the necessity of going deeply into debt to furnish relief to the needy. The law will flatten out the peaks and valleys of deflation and of inflation. It is, in short, a law that will take care of human needs and at the same time provide for the United States an economic structure of vastly greater soundness.

I congratulate all of you ladies and gentlemen, all of you in the Congress, in the executive departments and all of you who come from private life, and I thank you for your splendid efforts in behalf of this sound, needed and patriotic legislation.

If the Senate and the House of Representatives in this long and arduous session had done nothing more than pass this Bill, the session would be regarded as historic for all time.[6]

THE NEW DEAL RENEWED

As he accepted renomination for a second term, FDR sought to anticipate and outflank many groups on the Left by incorporating some of their proposals in his own program. Moreover, the earlier period of amicable relations with Big Business was over, for the now defunct NRA had resulted in ill feelings between the Administration and many businessmen. FDR's more militant attitude towards business was reflected in his speech at the Democratic national convention at Philadelphia, in 1936, in which he castigated "economic royalists." FDR's militant tone can be instructively compared with his earlier emphasis on mutual cooperation.

[6] *The New York Times,* August 15, 1935, a day after FDR signed the Social Security Act.

Senator Robinson, Members of the Democratic Convention, my friends:

Here, and in every community throughout the land, we are met at a time of great moment to the future of the Nation. It is an occasion to be dedicated to the simple and sincere expression of an attitude toward problems, the determination of which will profoundly affect America.

I come not only as a leader of a party, not only as a candidate for high office, but as one upon whom many critical hours have imposed and still impose a grave responsibility.

For the sympathy, help and confidence with which Americans have sustained me in my task I am grateful. For their loyalty I salute the members of our great party, in and out of political life in every part of the Union. I salute those of other parties, especially those in the Congress of the United States who on so many occasions have put partisanship aside. I thank the Governors of the several States, their Legislatures, their State and local officials who participated unselfishly and regardless of party in our efforts to achieve recovery and destroy abuses. Above all I thank the millions of Americans who have borne disaster bravely and have dared to smile through the storm.

America will not forget these recent years, will not forget that the rescue was not a mere party task. It was the concern of all of us. In our strength we rose together, rallied our energies together, applied the old rules of common sense, and together survived.

In those days we feared fear. That was why we fought fear. And today, my friends, we have won against the most dangerous of our foes. We have conquered fear.

But I cannot, with candor, tell you that all is well with the world. Clouds of suspicion, tides of ill-will and intolerance gather darkly in many places. In our own land we enjoy indeed a fullness of life greater than that of most Nations. But the rush of modern civilization itself has raised for us new difficulties, new problems which must be solved if we are to preserve to the United States the political and economic freedom for which Washington and Jefferson planned and fought.

Philadelphia is a good city in which to write American history. This is fitting ground on which to reaffirm the faith of our fathers; to pledge ourselves to restore to the people a wider freedom; to give to 1936 as the founders gave to 1776—an American way of life.

That very word freedom, in itself and of necessity, suggests freedom from some restraining power. In 1776 we sought freedom from the tyranny of a political autocracy—from the eighteenth century royalists who held special privileges from the crown. It was to perpetuate their privilege that they governed without the consent of the governed; that they denied the right of free assembly and free-speech; that they restricted the worship of God; that they put the average man's property and the average man's life in pawn to the mercenaries of dynastic power; that they regimented the people.

And so it was to win freedom from the tyranny of political autocracy that the American Revolution was fought. That victory gave the business of governing into the hands of the average man, who won the right with his neighbors to make and order his own destiny through his own Government. Political tyranny was wiped out at Philadelphia on July 4, 1776.

Since that struggle, however, man's inventive genius released new forces in our land which reordered the lives of our people. The age of machinery, of railroads, of steam and electricity; the telegraph and the radio; mass production, mass distribution—all of these combined to bring forward a new civilization and with it a new problem for those who sought to remain free.

For out of this modern civilization economic royalists carved new dynasties. New kingdoms were built upon concentration of control over material things. Through new uses of corporations, banks and securities, new machinery of industry and agriculture, of labor and capital—all undreamed of by the fathers—the whole structure of modern life was impressed into this royal service.

There was no place among this royalty for our many thousands of small business men and merchants who sought to make a worthy use of the American system of initiative and profit They were no more free than the worker or the farmer. Even honest and progressive-minded men of wealth, aware of their obligation to their generation, could never know just where they fitted into this dynastic scheme of things

It was natural and perhaps human that the privileged princes of these new economic dynasties, thirsting for power, reached out for control over Government itself. They created a new despotism and wrapped it in the robes of legal sanction. In its service new mercenaries sought to regiment the people, their labor, and their property. And as a result the average man once more confronts the problem that faced the Minute Man.

The hours men and women worked, the wages they received, the conditions of their labor—these had passed beyond the control of the people, and were imposed by this new industrial dictatorship. The savings of the average family, the capital of the small business man, the investments set aside for old age—other people's money—these were tools which the new economic royalty used to dig itself in.

Those who tilled the soil no longer reaped the rewards which were their right. The small measure of their gains was decreed by men in distant cities.

Throughout the Nation, opportunity was limited by monopoly. Individual initiative was crushed in the cogs of a great machine. The field open for free business was more and more restricted. Private enterprise, indeed, became too private. It became privileged enterprise, not free enterprise.

An old English judge once said: "Necessitous men are not free men." Liberty requires opportunity to make a living—a living decent according to the standard of the time, a living which gives man not only enough to live by, but something to live for.

For too many of us the political equality we once had won was meaningless in the face of economic inequality. A small group had concentrated into their own hands an almost complete control over other people's property, other people's money, other people's labor—other people's lives. For too many of us life was no longer free; liberty no longer real; men could no longer follow the pursuit of happiness.

Against economic tyranny such as this, the American citizen could appeal only to the organized power of Government. The collapse of 1929 showed up the despotism for what it was. The election of 1932 was the people's mandate to end it. Under that mandate it is being ended.

The royalists of the economic order have conceded that political freedom was the business of the Government, but they have maintained that economic slavery was nobody's business. They granted that the Government could protect the citizen in his right to vote, but they denied that the Government could do anything to protect the citizen in his right to work and his right to live.

Today we stand committed to the proposition that freedom is no half-and-half affair. If the average citizen is guaranteed equal opportunity in the polling place, he must have equal opportunity in the market place.

These economic royalists complain that we seek to overthrow the institutions of America. What they really complain of is that we seek to take away their power. Our allegiance to American institutions requires the overthrow of this kind of power. In vain they seek to hide behind the Flag and the Constitution. In their blindness they forget what the Flag and the Constitution stand for. Now, as always, they stand for democracy, not tyranny; for freedom, not subjection; and against a dictatorship by mob rule and the overprivileged alike. . . .

Governments can err, Presidents do make mistakes, but the immortal Dante tells us that divine justice weighs the sins of the cold-blooded and the sins of the warm-hearted in different scales.

Better the occasional faults of a Government that lives in a spirit of charity than the consistent omissions of a Government frozen in the ice of its own indifference.

There is a mysterious cycle in human events. To some generations much is given. Of other generations much is expected. This generation of Americans has a rendezvous with destiny.

In this world of ours in other lands, there are some people, who, in times past, have lived and fought for freedom, and seem to have grown too weary to carry on the fight. They have sold their heritage of freedom for the illusion of a living. They have yielded their democracy.

I believe in my heart that only our success can stir their ancient hope. They begin to know that here in America we are waging a great and successful war. It is not alone a war against want and destitution and economic demoralization. It is more than that; it is a war for the survival of democracy. We are fighting to save a great and precious form of government for ourselves and for the world.

I accept the commission you have tendered me. I join with you. I am enlisted for the duration of the war.[7]

THE NEGRO

FDR did little specifically to relieve Negro discontent. But New Deal welfare legislation was framed on an equalitarian basis: eligible workers, farmers, and businessmen were granted benefits regardless of color, although in the South the local administration of rural programs often followed traditional patterns of discrimination. Mrs. Roosevelt was especially active in working for Negro civil rights at a time of unquestioned segregation and brutal lynchings. Roosevelt's letter, though slightly patronizing, is politically tame.

My dear Bishop Wright:

I appreciate the opportunity of extending greetings to all those who are planning to participate in the celebration of the Seventy-fourth Anniversary of the issuance of the Preliminary Proclamation of Emancipation by President Lincoln.

It is an occasion for recalling the great progress which Negroes have made as citizens of our Republic. It also is an occasion for remembering that in the truest sense freedom cannot be bestowed, it must be achieved;

[7] *The New York Times,* June 28, 1936.

and that there must be constant vigilance if it is to be maintained. The record which our Negro citizens have made in their own personal and racial development and their contribution to the material advancement of our country and to the promotion of its ideals are well known.

I heartily congratulate them on their record, and hope that in the future, as in the past, they will continue to show intelligence, industry and fortitude in striving for the best our Democracy offers.

Very sincerely yours,[8]

BATTLE WITH THE SUPREME COURT: FIRESIDE CHAT OF 1937

Perhaps one of FDR's greatest political defeats came in 1937 with his unsuccessful battle to reform the United States Supreme Court. During 1935 a majority of the Justices struck down as unconstitutional various important New Deal measures, including the NRA and the AAA. Emboldened by his overwhelming election victory at the polls in 1936, FDR was determined to reform the court and to appoint Justices who would be favorable to his programs. The legislation he proposed was designed not merely to enlarge the Court but to force the retirement of Justices over 70, many of whom were hostile to the New Deal. In view of the importance which FDR attached to his court reform plan, he decided to devote a Fireside Chat exclusively to this question, part of which is reproduced below.

Last Thursday I described in detail certain economic problems which everyone admits now face the Nation. For the many messages which have come to me after that speech, and which it is physically impossible to answer individually, I take this means of saying "thank you."

Tonight, sitting at my desk in the White House, I make my first radio report to the people in my second term of office.

I am reminded of that evening in March, four years ago, when I made my first radio report to you. We were then in the midst of the great banking crisis.

Soon after, with the authority of the Congress, we asked the Nation to turn over all of its privately held gold, dollar for dollar, to the Government of the United States.

Today's recovery proves how right that policy was.

But when, almost two years later, it came before the Supreme Court its

[8] *The New York Times*, September 22, 1936.

constitutionality was upheld only by a five-to-four vote. The change of one vote would have thrown all the affairs of this great Nation back into hopeless chaos. In effect, four Justices ruled that the right under a private contract to exact a pound of flesh was more sacred than the main objectives of the Constitution to establish an enduring Nation.

In 1933 you and I knew that we must never let our economic system get completely out of joint again—that we could not afford to take the risk of another great depression.

We also became convinced that the only way to avoid a repetition of those dark days was to have a government with power to prevent and to cure the abuses and the inequalities which had thrown that system out of joint.

We then began a program of remedying those abuses and inequalities —to give balance and stability to our economic system—to make it bomb-proof against the causes of 1929.

Today we are only part-way through that program—and recovery is speeding up to a point where the dangers of 1929 are again becoming possible, not this week or month perhaps, but within a year or two.

National laws are needed to complete that program. Individual or local or state effort alone cannot protect us in 1937 any better than ten years ago.

It will take time—and plenty of time—to work out our remedies administratively even after legislation is passed. To complete our program of protection in time, therefore, we cannot delay one moment in making certain that our National Government has power to carry through.

Four years ago action did not come until the eleventh hour. It was almost too late.

If we learned anything from the depression we will not allow ourselves to run around in new circles of futile discussion and debate, always postponing the day of decision.

The American people have learned from the depression. For in the last three national elections an overwhelming majority of them voted a mandate that the Congress and the President begin the task of providing that protection—not after long years of debate, but now.

The Courts, however, have cast doubts on the ability of the elected Congress to protect us against catastrophe by meeting squarely our modern social and economic conditions.

We are at a crisis in our ability to proceed with that protection. It is a quiet crisis. There are no lines of depositors outside closed banks. But to the far-sighted it is far-reaching in its possibilities of injury to America.

I want to talk with you very simply about the need for present action in this crisis—the need to meet the unanswered challenge of one-third of a Nation ill-nourished, ill-clad, ill-housed.

Last Thursday I described the American form of Government as a three horse team provided by the Constitution to the American people so that their field might be plowed. The three horses are, of course, the three branches of government—the Congress, the Executive and the Courts. Two of the horses are pulling in unison today; the third is not. Those who have intimated that the President of the United States is trying to drive that team, overlook the simple fact that the President, as Chief Executive, is himself one of the three horses.

It is the American people themselves who are in the driver's seat.

It is the American people themselves who want the furrow plowed.

It is the American people themselves who expect the third horse to pull in unison with the other two.

I hope that you have re-read the Constitution of the United States in these past few weeks. Like the Bible, it ought to be read again and again.

In the last four years the sound rule of giving statutes the benefit of all reasonable doubt has been cast aside. The Court has been acting not as a judicial body, but as a policy-making body.

When the Congress has sought to stabilize national agriculture, to improve the conditions of labor, to safeguard business against unfair competition, to protect our national resources, and in many other ways, to serve our clearly national needs, the majority of the Court has been assuming the power to pass on the wisdom of these Acts of the Congress—and to approve or disapprove the public policy written into these laws.

That is not only my accusation. It is the accusation of most distinguished Justices of the present Supreme Court. I have not the time to quote to you all the language used by dissenting Justices in many of these cases. But in the case holding the Railroad Retirement Act unconstitutional, for instance, Chief Justice Hughes said in a dissenting opion that the majority opinion was "a departure from sound principles," and placed "an unwarranted limitation upon the commerce clause." And three other Justices agreed with him.

In the case holding the AAA unconstitutional, Justice Stone said of the majority opinion that it was a "tortured construction of the Constitution." And two other justices agreed with him.

In the case holding the New York Minimum Wage Law unconstitutional, Justice Stone said that the majority were actually reading into the Constitution their own "personal economic predilections," and that if the legislative power is not left free to choose the methods of solving the problems of poverty, subsistence and health of large numbers in the community, then "government is to be rendered impotent." And two other Justices agreed with him.

In the face of these dissenting opinions, there is no basis for the claim made by some members of the Court that something in the Constitution has compelled them regretfully to thwart the will of the people.

In the face of such dissenting opinions, it is perfectly clear, that as Chief Justice Hughes has said: "We are under a Constitution, but the Constitution is what the Judges say it is."

The Court in addition to the proper use of its judicial functions has improperly set itself up as a third House of Congress—a super-legislature, as one of the justices has called it—reading into the Constitution words and implications which are not there, and which were never intended to be there.

We have, therefore, reached the point as a Nation where we must take action to save the Constitution from the Court and the Court from itself. We must find a way to take an appeal from the Supreme Court to the Constitution itself. We want a Supreme Court which will do justice under the Constitution—not over it. In our Courts we want a government of laws and not of men.

I want—as all Americans want—an independent judiciary as proposed by the framers of the Constitution. That means a Supreme Court that will enforce the Constitution as written—that will refuse to amend the Constitution by the arbitrary exercise of judical power—amendment by judicial say-so. It does not mean a judiciary so independent that it can deny the existence of facts universally recognized.

How then could we proceed to perform the mandate given us? It was said in last year's Democratic platform, "If these problems cannot be effectively solved within the Constitution, we shall seek such clarifying amendments as will assure the power to enact those laws, adequately to regulate commerce, protect the public health and safety, and safeguard economic security." In other words, we said we would seek an amendment only if every other possible means by legislation were to fail.

When I commenced to review the situation with the problem squarely before me, I came by a process of elimination to the conclusion that, short of amendments, the only method which was clearly constitutional, and would at the same time carry out other much needed reforms, was to infuse new blood into all our Courts. We must have men worthy and equipped to carry out impartial justice. But, at the same time, we must have Judges who will bring to the Courts a present-day sense of the Constitution—Judges who will retain in the Courts the judicial functions of a court, and reject the legislative powers which the courts have today assumed.

In forty-five out of the forty-eight States of the Union, Judges are chosen not for life but for a period of years. In many States Judges must retire at the age of seventy. Congress has provided financial security by offering life pensions at full pay for Federal Judges on all Courts who are willing to retire at seventy. In the case of Supreme Court Justices, that pension is twenty thousand dollars a year. But all Federal Judges, once appointed, can, if they choose, hold office for life, no matter how old they may get to be.

What is my proposal? It is simply this: whenever a Judge or Justice of any Federal Court has reached the age of seventy and does not avail himself of the opportunity to retire on a pension, a new member shall be appointed by the President then in office, with the approval, as required by the Constitution, of the Senate of the United States.

That plan has two chief purposes. By bringing into the judicial system a steady and continuing stream of new and younger blood, I hope, first, to make the administration of all Federal justice speedier and, therefore, less costly; secondly, to bring to the decision of social and economic problems younger men who have had personal experience and contact with modern facts and circumstances under which average men have to live and work. This plan will save our national Constitution from hardening of the judicial arteries.

The number of Judges to be appointed would depend wholly on the decision of present Judges now over seventy, or those who would subsequently reach the age of seventy.

If, for instance, any one of the six Justices of the Supreme Court now over the age of seventy should retire as provided under the plan, no additional place would be created. Consequently, although there never can be more than fifteen, there may be only fourteen, or thirteen, or twelve. And there may be only nine.

There is nothing novel or radical about this idea. It seeks to maintain the Federal bench in full vigor. It has been discussed and approved by many persons of high authority ever since a similar proposal passed the House of Representatives in 1869.

Why was the age fixed at seventy? Because the laws of many States, the practice of the Civil Service, the regulations of the Army and Navy, and the rules of many of our Universities and of almost every great private business enterprise, commonly fix the retirement age at seventy years or less.

Those opposing this plan have sought to arouse prejudice and fear by crying that I am seeking to "pack" the Supreme Court and that a baneful precedent will be established.

What do they mean by the words "packing the Court"?

Let me answer this question with a bluntness that will end all honest misunderstanding of my purposes.

If by that phrase, "packing the court," it is charged that I wish to place on the bench spineless puppets who would disregard the law and would decide specific cases as I wished them to be decided, I make this answer— that no President fit for his office would appoint, and no Senate of honorable men fit for their office would confirm, that kind of appointees to the Supreme Court.

But, if by that phrase the charge is made that I would appoint and the Senate would confirm justices worthy to sit beside present members of the court who understand those modern conditions that I will appoint justices who will not undertake to override the judgment of the Congress on legislative policy—that I will appoint justices who will act as justices and not as legislators—if the appointment of such justices can be called "packing the courts," then I say that I and with me the vast majority of the American people favor doing just that thing—now.

Is it a dangerous precedent for the Congress to change the number of the justices? The Congress has always had, and will have, that power. The number of justices has been changed several times before—in the administrations of John Adams and Thomas Jefferson, both signers of the Declaration of Independence—Andrew Jackson, Abraham Lincoln, and Ulysses S. Grant.

I suggest only the addition of justices to the bench in accordance with a clearly defined principle relating to a clearly defined age limit. Fundamentally, if in the future, America cannot trust the Congress it elects to refrain from abuse of our constitutional usages, democracy will have failed far beyond the importance to it of any kind of precedent concerning the judiciary. . . .

This plan of mine is no attack on the court; it seeks to restore the court to its rightful and historic place in our system of constitutional government and to have it resume its high task of building anew on the Constitution "a system of living law." . . .

During the past half century the balance of power between the three great branches of the Federal Government has been tipped out of balance by the courts in direct contradiction of the high purposes of the framers of the Constitution. It is my purpose to restore that balance. You who know me will accept my solemn assurance that in a world in which democracy is under attack I seek to make American democracy succeed.[9]

DIPLOMATIST: GOOD NEIGHBOR

During his first Administration FDR sought, in diverse ways, to base his foreign policy on the principle of the Good Neighbor. But domestic problems were so pressing that the President could devote only a portion of his time to international events. By 1936, however, world tensions had increased to such an extent that the Good Neighbor policy in itself seemed ineffective in achieving its prime aim: international good-will and cooperation. After four years, thus, FDR considered in the following speech before a joint session of Congress whether it had become necessary to alter the principle upon which he had based foreign policy during his first term in the White House.

Mr. President, Mr. Speaker, Members of the Senate and of the House of Representatives:

We are about to enter upon another year of the responsibility which the electorate of the United States has placed in our hands. Having come so far, it is fitting that we should pause to survey the ground which we have covered and the path which lies ahead.

On the fourth day of March, 1933, on the occasion of taking the oath of office as President of the United States, I addressed the people of our country. Need I recall either the scene or the national circumstances attending the occasion? The crisis of that moment was almost exclusively a national one. In recognition of the fact, so obvious to the millions in the streets and in the homes of America, I devoted by far the greater part of that address to what I called, and the Nation called, critical days within our own borders.

You will remember that on that fourth of March, 1933, the world picture was an image of substantial peace. International consultation and widespread hope for the bettering of relations between the Nations gave to all of us a reasonable expectation that the barriers to mutual confidence, to increased trade, and to the peaceful settlement of disputes could be progressively removed. In fact, my only reference to the field of world policy in that address was in these words: "I would dedicate this Nation

[9] *The New York Times,* March 10, 1937.

to the policy of the good neighbor—the neighbor who resolutely respects himself and, because he does so, respects the rights of others—a neighbor who respects his obligations and respects the sanctity of his agreements in and with a world of neighbors."

In the years that have followed, that sentiment has remained the dedication of this Nation. Among the Nations of the great Western Hemisphere the policy of the good neighbor has happily prevailed. At no time in the four and a half centuries of modern civilization in the Americas has there existed—in any year, in any decade, in any generation in all that time—a greater spirit of mutual understanding, of common helpfulness, and of devotion to the ideals of self-government than exists today in the twenty-one American Republics and their neighbor, the Dominion of Canada. This policy of the good neighbor among the Americas is no longer a hope, no longer an objective remaining to be accomplished. It is a fact, active, present, pertinent and effective. In this achievement, every American Nation takes an understanding part. There is neither war, nor rumor of war, nor desire for war. The inhabitants of this vast area, two hundred and fifty million strong, spreading more than eight thousand miles from the Arctic to the Antarctic, believe in, and propose to follow, the policy of the good neighbor. They wish with all their heart that the rest of the world might do likewise.

The rest of the world—Ah! there is the rub.

Were I today to deliver an Inaugural Address to the people of the United States, I could not limit my comments on world affairs to one paragraph. With much regret I should be compelled to devote the greater part to world affairs. Since the summer of that same year of 1933, the temper and the purposes of the rulers of many of the great populations in Europe and in Asia have not pointed the way either to peace or to good-will among men. Not only have peace and good-will among men grown more remote in those areas of the earth during this period, but a point has been reached where the people of the Americas must take cognizance of growing ill-will, of marked trends toward aggression, of increasing armaments, of shortening tempers—a situation which has in it many of the elements that lead to the tragedy of general war.

On those other continents many Nations, principally the smaller peoples, if left to themselves, would be content with their boundaries and willing to solve within themselves and in cooperation with their neighbors their individual problems, both economic and social. The rulers of those Nations, deep in their hearts, follow these peaceful and reasonable aspirations of their peoples. These rulers must remain ever vigilant against the possibility today or tomorrow of invasion or attack by the rulers of other peoples who fail to subscribe to the principles of bettering the human race by peaceful means.

Within those other Nations—those which today must bear the primary, definite responsibility for jeopardizing world peace—what hope lies? To say the least, there are grounds for pessimism. It is idle for us or for others to preach that the masses of the people who constitute those Nations which are dominated by the twin spirits of autocracy and aggression, are out of sympathy with their rulers, that they are allowed no opportunity to express themselves, that they would change things if they could.

That, unfortunately, is not so clear. It might be true that the masses of the people in those Nations would change the policies of their Governments if they could be allowed full freedom and full access to the processes of democratic government as we understand them. But they do not have that access; lacking it they follow blindly and fervently the lead of those who seek autocratic power.

Nations seeking expansion, seeking the rectification of injustices springing from former wars, or seeking outlets for trade, for population or even for their own peaceful contributions to the progress of civilization, fail to demonstrate that patience necessary to attain reasonable and legitimate objectives by peaceful negotiation or by an appeal to the finer instincts of world justice.

They have therefore impatiently reverted to the old belief in the law of the sword, or to the fantastic conception that they, and they alone, are chosen to fulfill a mission and that all the others among the billion and a half of human beings in the world must and shall learn from and be subject to them.

I recognize and you will recognize that these words which I have chosen with deliberation will not prove popular in any Nation that chooses to fit this shoe to its foot. Such sentiments, however, will find sympathy and understanding in those Nations where the people themselves are honestly desirous of peace but must constantly align themselves on one side or the other in the kaleidoscopic jockeying for position which is characteristic of European and Asiatic relations today. For the peace-loving Nations, and there are many of them, find that their very identity depends on their moving and moving again on the chess board of international politics.

But the policy of the United States has been clear and consistent. We have sought with earnestness in every possible way to limit world armaments and to attain the peaceful solution of disputes among all Nations.

We have sought by every legitimate means to exert our moral influence against repression, against intolerance, against autocracy and in favor of freedom of expression, equality before the law, religious tolerance and popular rule.

In the field of commerce we have undertaken to encourage a more reasonable interchange of the world's goods. In the field of international finance we have, so far as we are concerned, put an end to dollar diplomacy, to money grabbing, to speculation for the benefit of the powerful and the rich, at the expense of the small and the poor.

As a consistent part of a clear policy, the United States is following a twofold neutrality toward any and all Nations which engage in wars that are not of immediate concern to the Americas. First, we decline to encourage the prosecution of war by permitting belligerents to obtain arms, ammunition or implements of war from the United States. Second, we seek to discourage the use by belligerent Nations of any and all American products calculated to facilitate the prosecution of a war in quantities over and above our normal exports of them in time of peace.

I trust that these objectives thus clearly and unequivocally stated will be carried forward by cooperation between this Congress and the President.[10]

QUARANTINE OF FOREIGN AGGRESSORS

By 1937 he was particularly concerned with the aggressive policies of Germany in Europe, and of Japan in the Far East. His growing apprehension was openly expressed in the "Quarantine Speech" of October 5, 1937, excerpted below, in which he advocated defensive measures to safeguard American security.

Mayor Kelly, Governor Horner, my friends in Chicago:

. . . It is because the people of the United States must, for the sake of their own future, give thought to the rest of the world, that I, as the responsible executive head of the Nation, have chosen this great inland city and this gala occasion to speak to you on a subject of definite national importance.

The political situation in the world, which of late has been growing progressively worse, is such as to cause grave concern and anxiety to all the peoples and nations who wish to live in peace and amity with their neighbors.

[10] *The New York Times*, January 4, 1936.

Some fifteen years ago the hopes of mankind for a continuing era of international peace were raised to great heights when more than sixty nations solemnly pledged themselves not to resort to arms in furtherance of their national aims and policies. The high aspirations expressed in the Briand-Kellogg Peace Pact and the hopes for peace thus raised have of late given way to a haunting fear of calamity. The present reign of terror and international lawlessness began a few years ago.

It began through unjustified interference in the internal affairs of other nations or the invasion of alien territory in violation of treaties. It has now reached a stage where the very foundations of civilization are seriously threatened. The landmarks, the traditions which have marked the progress of civilization toward a condition of law and order and justice are being wiped away.

Without a declaration of war and without warning or justification of any kind civilians, including vast numbers of women and children, are being ruthlessly murdered with bombs from the air. In times of so-called peace ships are being attacked and sunk by submarines without cause or notice. Nations are fomenting and taking sides in civil warfare in nations that have never done them any harm. Nations claiming freedom for themselves deny it to others.

Innocent peoples, innocent nations are being cruelly sacrificed to a greed for power and supremacy which is devoid of all sense of justice and humane consideration.

To paraphrase a recent author "perhaps we foresee a time when men, exultant in the technique of homicide, will rage so hotly over the world that every precious thing will be in danger, every book, every picture, every harmony, every treasure garnered through two millenniums, the small, the delicate, the defenseless—all will be lost or wrecked or utterly destroyed."

If those things come to pass in other parts of the world, let no one imagine that America will escape, that America may expect mercy, that this Western Hemisphere will not be attacked and that it will continue tranquilly and peacefully to carry on the ethics and the arts of civilization.

No, if those days come "there will be no safety by arms, no help from authority, no answer in science. The storm will rage till every flower of culture is trampled and all human beings are leveled in a vast chaos."

If those days are not to come to pass—if we are to have a world in which we can breathe freely and live in amity without fear—then the peace-loving nations must make a concerted effort to uphold laws and principles on which alone peace can rest secure.

The peace-loving nations must make a concerted effort in opposition to those violations of treaties and those ignorings of humane instincts which today are creating a state of international anarchy, international instability from which there is no escape through mere isolation or neutrality.

Those who cherish their freedom and recognize and respect the equal rights of their neighbors to be free and live in peace, must work together for the triumph of law and moral principles in order that peace, justice and confidence may prevail throughout the world. There must be a return to a belief in the pledged word, in the value of a signed treaty. There must be recognition of the fact that national morality is as vital as private morality.

The overwhelming majority of all the peoples and nations of the world today want to live in peace. They seek the removal of barriers against trade. They want to exert themselves in industry, in agriculture, in business, that they may increase their wealth through the production of wealth-producing goods rather than striving to produce military planes and bombs and machine guns and cannon for the destruction of human lives and useful property.

In those nations of the world which seem to be piling armament on armament for purposes of aggression, and those other nations which fear acts of aggression against them and their security, a very high proportion of their national income is being spent directly for armaments. It runs from thirty to as high as fifty percent in most of those cases.

We are fortunate. The proportion that we spend in the United States is far less—eleven or twelve percent.

How happy we are that the circumstances of the moment permit us to put our money into bridges and boulevards, dams and reforestation, the conservation of our soil and many other kinds of useful works rather than into huge standing armies and vast supplies of implements of war.

Nevertheless, my friends, I am compelled and you are compelled to look ahead. The peace, the freedom, the security of ninety percent of the population of the world is being jeopardized by the remaining ten percent who are threatening a breakdown of all international order and law. Surely the ninety percent who want to live in peace under law and in accordance with moral standards that have received almost universal acceptance through the centuries, can and must find some way to make their will prevail.

Yes, the situation is definitely of universal concern. The questions involved relate not merely to violations of specific provisions of particular treaties; they are questions of war and peace, of international law and especially of principles of humanity. It is true that they involve definite violations of agreements, and especially of the Covenant of the League of Nations, the Briand-Kellogg Pact and the Nine Power Treaty. And we have signed both of the last two. But they involve also problems of world economy, world security and world humanity.

It seems to be unfortunately true that the epidemic of world lawlessness is spreading.

And mark this well! When an epidemic of physical disease starts to spread, the community approves and joins in a quarantine of the patients in order to protect the health of the community against the spread of the disease.

It is my determination to pursue a policy of peace. It is my determination to adopt every practicable measure to avoid involvement in war. It ought to be inconceivable that in this modern era, and in the face of experience, any nation could be so foolish and ruthless as to run the risk of plunging the whole world into war by invading and violating in contravention of solemn treaties, the territory of other nations that have done them no real harm and which are too weak to protect themselves adequately. Yet the peace of the world and the welfare and security of every nation, including our own, is today being threatened by that very thing.

No nation which refuses to exercise forbearance and to respect the freedom and rights of others can long remain strong and retain the confidence and respect of other nations. No nation ever loses its dignity or its good standing by conciliating its differences, and by exercising great patience, patience with, and consideration for, the rights of other nations.

War is a contagion, whether it be declared or undeclared. It can engulf states and peoples remote from the original scene of hostilities. Yes, we are determined to keep out of war, yet we cannot insure ourselves against the disastrous effects of war and the dangers of involvement. We are adopting such measures as will minimize our risk of involvement but we cannot have complete protection in a world of disorder in which confidence and security have broken down.

If civilization is to survive the principles of the Prince of Peace must be restored. Shattered trust between nations must be revived.

Most important of all, the will for peace on the part of peace-loving nations must express itself to the end that nations that may be tempted to violate their agreements and the rights of others will desist from such a cause. There must be positive endeavors to preserve peace.

America hates war. America hopes for peace. Therefore, America actively engages in the search for peace.[11]

[11] *The New York Times,* October 6, 1937.

LEND-LEASE PRESS CONFERENCE, DECEMBER 17, 1940

On September 1, 1939, Germany attacked, and within a few weeks, conquered Poland; Britain and France declared war in support of their ally; by June, 1940, Germany had captured Norway, Denmark, Belgium, Holland, and occupied most of France. Only Britain, protected for a time by her island security, stood against Hitler. British Prime Minister, Winston Churchill, pleaded with FDR for more and more weapons and supplies. But as British needs increased, her economic resources declined. Roosevelt devised Lend-Lease as a means of assisting Britain without cash payment. ("I am trying . . . to get rid of the silly, foolish, old dollar sign.") Churchill later described FDR's scheme as being "the single most unselfish act in history by one state for another." A portion of the report about a press conference at which FDR discussed Lend-Lease is included below.

In the present world situation, there was no doubt in the minds of an overwhelming number of Americans that the best immediate defense of the United States is the success of Great Britain in defending herself. Quite aside from our historic and current interest in the survival of democracy, therefore, it is important from the selfish viewpoint of American defense that we should do everything to help the British Empire defend itself.

He had read a great deal of nonsense about finances in the past few days by people who could think only in traditional terms. No major war was ever won or lost through lack of money. . . .

Now in speeches and stories, the same attitude is being expressed in this war. This is wrong. It is not merely a matter of doing things in the traditional way. Additional production facilities—factories, ship-building ways, munitions plants, etc.—are most important to the United States.

Talking selfishly, from the viewpoint of American defense, orders from Great Britain are a tremendous asset because they automatically create additional facilities. There are several ways of encouraging this. Narrow-minded men assumed that the only way was to repeal certain statutes like the Neutrality Act and the Johnson Act (prohibiting loans to nations whose war debts are in default) and then lend money either through private banks or the government.

That is the banal type of mind. There is another, also somewhat banal, that suggests outright cash gifts (although we might come to it). . . . It was not at all certain that this was necessary, or that Britain, which had her amour propre would accept a gift from the American taxpayers. One had to place one's self in the other man's shoes.

There are other ways and these are now being explored. This exploration has been proceeding for three or four weeks. The essential thing is to increase our production facilities and the flow of supplies to Great Britain. The following is put up as one of several plans that might be devised.

It is possible for the United States to take over British orders, and because they are essentially the same kind of munitions we use ourselves, turn them into American orders. We have enough money to do it. Thereafter, such portion of them as military events would determine to be right and proper would be allowed to go to the other side. The materials could either be leased or sold subject to mortgage to the people on the other side of the ocean.

This is in line with the idea that the best possible defense of Great Britain is the best defense of the United States. The materials would be more useful in Great Britain than if kept in storage here. What the President was trying to do was eliminate the silly-fool dollar sign, and that was something brand-new. . . .

Suppose the house of the President's neighbor catches fire and he has a length of garden hose, 400 or 500 feet. If he can take the hose and connect it to the neighbor's hydrant, he may be able to put out the fire. He does not say his hose cost $15; pay me $15. He doesn't want $15, but his hose back when the fire is over. The neighbor gives back the hose and pays him for the use of it. If it gets smashed in the fire, the President says he was glad to lend it. The neighbor says he will replace the part destroyed. If the President has got back his hose, he has done a pretty good job.

The broad thought in this connection is that if we take over not all but a large part of future British war orders when they come off the production line and come to an arrangement for their use by the British and get repaid in kind when the war is over, that would be satisfactory. We would leave out the dollar mark in the transaction, whether it dealt with guns, planes or merchant ships, substituting a gentleman's agreement to pay in kind.[12]

THE FALA SPEECH

The 1944 Republican presidential candidate, Governor Thomas E. Dewey of New York, criticized FDR's handling of the war as both

[12] *The New York Times,* December 18, 1940.

wasteful and corrupt. Charges of nepotism were made—two of Roosevelt's sons were officers of fairly high rank. There were many people, Roosevelt commented, who hoped that the United States would win, but that he would lose, the war. Early in October, in a carefully planned address to the Teamsters Union, Roosevelt delivered his finest political address. After the speech someone remarked: "From now on the American people will consider this as a contest of Dewey versus Fala."

The whole purpose of Republican oratory these days seems to be to switch labels. . . .

Can the Old Guard pass itself off as the New Deal?

I think not.

We have all seen many marvelous stunts in the circus but no performing elephant could turn a handspring without falling flat on his back. . . .

What the Republican leaders are now saying in effect is this: "Oh just forget what we used to say, we have changed our minds now—we have been reading the public opinion polls about these things and now we know what the American people want." And they say: "Don't leave the task of making peace to those old men who first urged it, and who have already laid the foundations for it, and who have had to fight all of us inch by inch during the last five years to do it. Why, just turn it all over to us. We'll do it so skillfully—that we won't lose a single isolationist vote or a single isolationist campaign contribution. . . .

Now, there is an old and somewhat lugubrious adage that says: "Never speak of rope in the house of a man who has been hanged." In the same way, if I were a Republican leader speaking to a mixed audience, the last word in the whole dictionary that I think I would use is that word "depression." . . .

These Republican leaders have not been content with attacks on me, or my wife, or my sons. No, not content with that, they now include my little dog, Fala. Well, of course, I don't resent attacks, and my family doesn't resent attacks, but Fala does resent attacks. You know, Fala is Scotch, and being a Scottie, as soon as he learned that the Republican fiction writers in Congress and out had concocted a story that I had left him behind on the Aleutian Islands and had sent a destroyer back to find him—at a cost to the taxpayers of two or three, or eight or twenty million dollars—his Scotch soul was furious. He has not been the same dog since. I am accustomed to hearing malicious falsehoods about myself—such as that old, worm-eaten chestnut that I have represented myself as indispensable. But I think I have a right to resent, to object to libelous statements about my dog.[13]

YALTA: ROOSEVELT AT WAR

Roosevelt, Churchill, and Stalin held diplomatic and strategic conferences twice during the war: at Teheran, in late 1943 and at Yalta in February, 1945. Both conferences demonstrated the tension and exasperation provoked when temporary allies, with often competing interests, worked toward a common goal: the defeat of the Axis powers. The report of the Yalta meeting below is excerpted from Charles Bohlen's minutes of a Tripartite Dinner at the Yusupov Palace, Yalta, Russia.

The atmosphere of the dinner was most cordial, and forty-five toasts in all were drunk.* Marshal Stalin was in an excellent humor and even in high spirits. Most of the toasts were routine—to the armed forces of the representative countries and the military leaders and the continuing friendship of the three great powers.

Marshal Stalin proposed a toast to the health of the Prime Minister, who [sic] he characterized as the bravest governmental figure in the world. He said that due in large measure to Mr. Churchill's courage and staunchness, England, when she stood alone, had divided the might of Hitlerite Germany at a time when the rest of Europe was falling flat on its face before Hitler. He said that Great Britain, under Mr. Churchill's leadership, had carried on the fight alone irrespective of existing or potential allies. The Marshal concluded that he knew of few examples in history where the courage of one man had been so important to the future history of the world. He drank a toast to Mr. Churchill, his fighting friend and a brave man.

The Prime Minister, in his reply, toasted Marshal Stalin as the mighty leader of a mighty country, which had taken the full shock of the German war machine, had broken its back and had driven the tyrants from her soil. He said he knew that in peace no less than in war Marshal Stalin would continue to lead his people from success to success.

Marshal Stalin then proposed the health of the President of the United

[13] *The New York Times*, September 24, 1944.
* [Each leader brought ten guests from his advisory staff. Ed.]

States. He said that he and Mr. Churchill in their respective countries had had relatively simple decisions. They had been fighting for their very existence against Hitlerite Germany but there was a third man whose country had not been seriously threatened with invasion, but who had had perhaps a broader conception of national interest and even though his country was not directly imperilled had been the chief forger of the instruments which had lead [sic] to the mobilization of the world against Hitler. He mentioned in this connection Lend-Lease as one of the President's most remarkable and vital achievements in the formation of the anti-Hitler combination and in keeping the Allies in the field against Hitler.

The President, in reply to this toast, said he felt the atmosphere at this dinner was as that of a family, and it was in those words that he liked to characterize the relations that existed between our three countries. He said that great changes had occurred in the world during the last three years, and even greater changes were to come. He said that each of the leaders represented here were working in their own way for the interests of their people. He said that fifty years ago there were vast areas of the world where people had little opportunity and no hope, but much had been accomplished, although there were still great areas where people had little opportunity and little hope, and their objectives here were to give to every man, woman and child on this earth the possibility of security and wellbeing.

In a subsequent toast to the alliance between the three great powers, Marshal Stalin remarked that it was not so difficult to keep unity in time of war since there was a joint aim to defeat the common enemy which was clear to everyone. He said the difficult task came after the war when diverse interests tended to divide the allies. He said he was confident that the present alliance would meet this test also and that it was our duty to see that it would, and that our relations in peacetime should be as strong as they had been in war.

The Prime Minister then said he felt we were all standing on the crest of a hill with the glories of future possibilities stretching before us. He said that in the modern world the function of leadership was to lead the people out from the forests into the broad sunlit plains of peace and happiness. He felt this prize was nearer our grasp than anytime before in history and it would be a tragedy for which history would never forgive us if we let this prize slip from our grasp through inertia or carelessness.

Justice Byrnes proposed a toast to the common man all over the world. He said there had been many toasts to leaders and officials and while we all shared these sentiments we should never forget the common man or woman who lives on this earth.

Miss Harriman, replying for the three ladies present, then proposed a toast to those who had worked so hard in the Crimea for our comfort, and having seen the destruction wrought by the Germans here she had fully realized what had been accomplished.[14]

[14] *Foreign Relations of the United States: The Conferences at Malta and Yalta, 1945* (Washington: 1955), pp. 797-799.

PART TWO

FDR OBSERVED

How did contemporaries assess FDR's character and aims? Since he was a many-sided individual perhaps no one person was ever able fully to fathom his personality. Yet some of the more astute observers were able at least to glimpse one or another aspect of his motivations. Many of his family and other close associates found it simpler to explain the causes of his actions before he became President than after—his life became still more complicated. Thus, until 1932 FDR's contemporaries found him to be a not too unusual country gentleman in politics, an able and likeable, but not extraordinary, individual. After 1932 contemporary assessments were much more varied. Some thought him to be a pragmatist, others found him an idealist, still others considered him to be a crass realist, while a few saw him as fulfilling a symbolic function in personifying the preservation of democracy. The selections in Part Two are intended to suggest some of the major strands in FDR's complex personality as they impressed those who knew him.

3

FDR's First Fifty Years

As already noted, contemporaries of FDR found much to admire in him before 1932, but few suspected him capable of greatness. Rather, they viewed him as an attractive and representative American aristocrat. The reminiscences of his mother, of Headmaster Endicott Peabody of Groton, of those who followed his career in the New York State Senate and as Assistant Secretary of the Navy, indicate this well. It was also evident in the reflections of Al Smith and the astute political leaders who surrounded him, who thought of FDR largely as a country squire, and little suspected the powers of leadership hidden within his character. The newspaper columnist Walter Lippmann expressed a not uncommon point of view when he wrote in 1932 that FDR was "a pleasant man who without any important qualifications for the post wanted very much to be President of the United States." The accounts of FDR which follow

illustrate the impressions which contemporaries had of him before he
became the nation's Chief Executive.

SARA DELANO ROOSEVELT: CHILDHOOD

*That FDR underwent a normal childhood and reflected no very
unusual or extraordinary traits was confirmed by those who knew
him well during this period. Although his mother embellished her
later reminiscences of him, nevertheless the normal progress of his
early years is still apparent in the following excerpt.*

Did I ever think when he was little that Franklin might be President? Never, oh never! That was the last thing I should ever have imagined for him, or that he should be in public life of any sort. I know that
traditionally every American mother believes her son will one day be
President, but much as I love tradition and believe in perpetuating good
ones, that is one to which I never happened to subscribe.

What was my ambition for him? Very simple—it might even be thought
not very ambitious, but to me, and to him, too, it was the highest ideal I
could hold up before our boy—to grow to be like his father, straight and
honorable, just and kind, an upstanding American.

We never tried, you see, his father and I, to influence him against his
own tastes and inclinations or to shape his life. At least we made every
effort not to and thought we were succeeding pretty well until one day,
when Franklin was only about five, we noticed that he seemed much depressed and bound, do what we would to amuse him, not to be distracted
from his melancholy. Finally, a little alarmed, I asked him whether he
was unhappy. He did not answer at once and then said very seriously,
"Yes, I am unhappy."

When I asked him why, he was again silent for a moment or two. Then
with a curious little gesture that combined entreaty with a suggestion of
impatience, he clasped his hands in front of him and exclaimed,
"Oh, for freedom!"

It seems funny now, but at the time I was honestly shocked. For all he
was such a child, his voice had a desperate note that made me realize how
seriously he meant it.

That night I talked it over with his father who, I confess, often told me
I nagged the boy. We agreed that unconsciously we had probably regu-
lated the child's life too closely, even though we knew he had ample time
for exercise and play. Evidently he was quite satisfied with what he did

with his time, but what worried him was the necessity of conforming to given hours.

So the very next morning I told him that he might do whatever he pleased that day. He need obey no former rules nor report at any given intervals, and he was allowed to roam at will. We paid no attention to him, and, I must say, he proved his desire for freedom by completely ignoring us. That evening, however, a very dirty, tired youngster came dragging in. He was hungry and ready for bed, but we did not ask him where he had been or what he had been doing. We could only deduce that his adventures had been a little lacking in glamour, for the next day, quite of his own accord, he went contentedly back to his routine.

* * *

And if they are half as easy to manage as Franklin was, when as a little tot we took him abroad, it will be no hardship, for it was a joy to take him about with us. Of course, like all small boys, he liked to get into all sorts of mischief, but he never did any real or lasting damage, although one day, during his first crossing—I think he was only two and a half at the time—he gave us pretty much of a fright.

It was during luncheon Franklin had raised his glass to take, as we thought, a swallow of water. Suddenly, to my horror, I discovered that he had bitten a large chunk of glass out of the side of the tumbler. I lost no time, as you can imagine, hustling him out of the room, where I fished about in terror for the dangerous mouthful. The jagged piece thrown into the sea where it could do no further harm, I lectured him severely and returned him, penitent, I felt certain, to the table. There, if you please, he picked up the goblet with which the steward had replaced the broken glass and pretended, an impish glint in his eyes, to give it the same treatment he had accorded the first.

"Franklin," I admonished him sternly, "where is your obedience?"

"My 'bedience," Franklin stated solemnly, "has gone upstairs for a walk." [1]

ENDICOTT PEABODY: GROTON

Headmaster Endicott Peabody of Groton also recalled in later years that as a schoolboy FDR had impressed faculty and students alike as an amiable, well adjusted, and quite unexceptionable and likeable youngster. The following excerpts are from a biography

[1] Sara Delano Roosevelt, *My Boy Franklin* (*As Told to Isabelle Leighton and Gabrielle Forash*) (New York, 1933), pp. 3-5.

of Peabody which includes several letters which refer to FDR's youth.

[December 19, 1932]

There has been a good deal written about Franklin Roosevelt when he was a boy at Groton, more than I should have thought justified by the impression that he left at the school. He was a quiet, satisfactory boy of more than ordinary intelligence, taking a good position in his Form, but not brilliant. Athletically he was rather too slight for success. We all liked him. So far as I know this is true of the masters and boys alike. I have always been fond of him. . . .[2]

[1936]

He was at Groton for four years, and so far as I remember there was no suspicion of untruthfulness or insincerity during his entire course; nor did I hear of anything against his reputation at Harvard University.[3]

JAMES ROOSEVELT: HARVARD

FDR's oldest son, James Roosevelt, in various reminiscences excerpted below, provided an intimate glimpse of his father's early life garnered from what he heard within the family circle as well as from his own observations. He remarked particularly upon the efforts of FDR's strong-minded mother to dominate her son, and wondered like many others how his father was able to escape this maternal influence.

The first American-born Roosevelt, from whom both Father's and Mother's branches of the family stemmed, was Nicholas, son of Claes Martenszen van Rosenvelt. Claes came to Nieuw Amsterdam—later New York—from Holland around 1649. From Nicholas' line, two Presidents—Theodore Roosevelt, who was Mother's uncle, and Father—were produced. Mother, blithely ignoring the fundamental conflict in the political affiliations of the two branches, sometimes quips that "the only difference between my side of the family and Franklin's is that the Oyster Bay

---

[2] Frank D. Ashburn, *Peabody of Groton* (New York: 1944), p. 341.
[3] *Ibid.*, p. 344.

Roosevelts are 'REW-sevelts,' and the Hyde Park Roosevelts are 'ROSE-evelts.' "

On Grandmother's side, Father was a Delano, a clan of Flemish descent which numbered in its company some swashbuckling sea captains, China traders, and other colorful characters. The first Delano—then de la Noye —in America was one Philippe, who arrived in the Massachusetts Bay Colony in 1621, much earlier, as Granny was fond of remarking, than the Johnny-come-lately Roosevelts. Our redoubtable grandmother considered her side of the family infinitely the superior of the two lines, and often commented, with the finality of a Supreme Court justice handing down an opinion, that "Franklin is a *Delano*, not a Roosevelt at all."

At heart, Father was as tradition-loving as any Daughter of the American Revolution—even though, as President, he once jolted that august society by reminding it that "you and I . . . are descended from immigrants and revolutionists." (That speech was delivered in 1938 when I was a White House secretary, and I've always regretted that I did not go along to hear him startle the good ladies.) The difference was that Father mixed his reverence with irreverence, and refused to be stuffy about his ancestors.[4]

Granny's volume provides an interesting, if rose-tinted, picture of Father's early life. I say "rose-tinted" advisedly; among other things, it contains the rather remarkable assertion: "We never tried . . . his father and I, to influence him against his own tastes and inclinations or to shape his life. . . ." She pictured him as a manly, precocious little fellow, and indignantly denied that he was "lonely" because he grew up as an only child. She admitted he was "spoiled"—not by her, of course, but by his adoring nurses.

But Granny revealed perhaps more than she realized about her possessive feelings toward her only son. She described how she and Grandfather came tearing home from Europe when Father came down with a bad case of scarlet fever which went into a period of prolonged complications. As visits were prohibited, Granny told how she circumvented the quarantine. "Several times each day," she related, "I would climb a tall, rickety ladder, and, by seating myself on the top, managed to see into the room and talk with our small, convalescent scapegrace. He loved to see me appear over the window ledge. . . ." Whenever I envision the commanding figure of my grandmother, clambering in rustling skirts up a shaky ladder to converse through a window with her little boy, I involuntarily steal one of Father's favorite phrases—"*I love it!*" I'm certain that's exactly what Father must have said when he read this passage of Granny's recollections.

[4] James Roosevelt, *Affectionately, F.D.R.* (New York, 1959), pp. 17-18.

As part of the pattern of Father's early life, he went to Europe eight times during his first fourteen years, shepherded by various governesses and tutors, and his parents. On his last trip, he bicycled through Germany with a tutor. He liked to boast to my brothers and me—presumably to prove to us that he had been a regular guy—that he had been arrested four times in one day for stealing cherries, wheeling his bike into the waiting room of a railroad station, pedaling into a town after sunset (*verboten*), and running over and killing a goose. As the years went by, he improved bit by bit on this story, finally insisting that the goose really had "committed suicide" by sticking its neck through the spokes. Our little brother, Johnny, must have remembered Pa's escapade, for, on his own memorable trip through Europe in 1937, in which a fast motorcar substituted for a bicycle, John wrote me: "We've had three casualties thus far on the road, all of them yesterday coming back from Budapest. The score now stands at two ducks, one chicken and thousands of furious peasants whom we made scatter to the fields by means of cut-out and siren. . . ."

In September, 1896—a bit behind schedule, for his mother was reluctant to let him leave the nest—Father entered Groton. "It is hard to leave our darling boy," Granny noted in her diary. "James and I feel this parting very much." There, under the guidance of the Reverend Doctor Endicott Peabody, who was to become a major influence in the spiritual and traditional side of Father's life, Father's personality was molded by the rigid pattern of discipline and respectability that dominated the Groton way of life. Conformity, a sense of obligation, and acceptance of that peculiar Grotonian tenet best described as "playing the game" seemingly came naturally to him.

After Groton, the natural progression was to Harvard. Even at Harvard, Father had the maternal influence with which to cope, for, after his father's death, his doting Mama—though she insists in her book that she abstained from interfering in his life—came to Cambridge to be near her cherished son.

To me, the miracle is that Father was strong enough in later life to rise above his Hyde Park-parental-Groton-Harvard background and to become such a human, sympathetic, understanding individual.[5]

ELEANOR ROOSEVELT: MARRIAGE

The atmosphere of FDR's youthful life amidst upper class society was well recalled by his wife as she described her wedding—one of

[5] *Ibid.*, pp. 20-22.

the great social events in New York of 1905—and also her domineering new mother-in-law.

The week before our wedding was all frantic haste. Some of my bridesmaids came to help me write notes of thanks for wedding presents, of course signing my name. One day we discovered to our horror that Isabella Selmes was writing "Franklin and I are so pleased with your gift, etc.," and then signing her own name instead of mine! The bridesmaids were dressed in cream taffeta with three feathers in their hair, and had tulle veils floating down their backs.

Franklin had a number of ushers, and Lathrop Brown was his best man. My own dress was heavy, stiff satin, with shirred tulle in the neck, and long sleeves. My Grandmother Hall's rose-point Brussels lace covered the dress, and a veil of the same lace fell from my head over my long train.

The three feathers worn by the bridesmaids were reminiscent of the Roosevelt crest, and Franklin had designed a tie pin for his ushers, with three little feathers in diamonds. He also designed and gave me a gold watch, with my initials in diamonds and a pin to wear it on with the three feathers, which I still wear, though watches dangling from pins are not so much the fashion today.

My mother-in-law had given me a dog-collar of pearls which I wore, feeling decked out beyond description. I carried a large bouquet of lilies of the valley.

The date chosen had an added significance to all my Hall family, for it was my mother's birthday.

March 17th arrived. Uncle Ted came to New York from Washington, he reviewed the parade, and then came to Cousin Susie's house, where Franklin and I were married.

Many of our guests had difficulty in reaching the house because of the parade which blocked the streets. No one could enter from Fifth Avenue, and the police guarded Uncle Ted so carefully it made it difficult for anyone to come in from Madison Avenue. A few irate guests arrived after the ceremony was over!

The ceremony was performed by the Reverend Endicott Peabody, the head of Groton School. My Cousin Susie's drawing room opened into her mother's house, so it gave us two large rooms. We were actually married in Mrs. Ludlow's house, where an altar had been arranged in front of the fireplace, just as had been done for Pussie's wedding the year before.

When the ceremony had been performed, we turned around to receive congratulations from the various members of our families and our friends.

In the meantime, Uncle Ted went into the library, where refreshments were served. Those closest to us did take time to wish us well, but the great majority of the guests were far more interested in the thought of being able to see and listen to the President—and in a very short time this young married couple were standing alone! The room in which the President was holding forth was filled with people laughing gaily at his stories, which were always amusing. I do not remember being particularly surprised by this, and I cannot remember that even Franklin seemed to mind. We simply followed the crowd and listened with the rest. Later we gathered together enough ushers and bridesmaids to cut the wedding cake, and I imagine we made Uncle Ted attend this ceremony. Then we went upstairs to dress. By this time the lion of the afternoon had left!

We left amidst the usual shower of rice. One old friend of mine had not been able to be at the wedding. Bob Ferguson was laid up with a fever, which ever since the Spanish War, when he had been one of Uncle Ted's "Rough Riders," came back at intervals, so before we went to our train we stopped in to see him and then took the train for Hyde Park, where we spent our first honeymoon. It is not customary to have two honeymoons, but we did, because my husband had to finish out his year at law school.

Our first home was a small apartment in a hotel in the West Forties in New York City for the remainder of the spring while Franklin continued his study of law.

It was lucky that my first housekeeping was so simple. I had a tiny room for Hall, so he could spend his Easter holiday with us, and he seemed to fill the entire apartment. Mending was all that was really required of me in the way of housewifely duties in those first few weeks, and fortunately I was well able to do that, thanks to Madeleine's training. But I knew less than nothing about even ordering meals, and what little I had learned at Tivoli before I went abroad to school had completely slipped out of my mind, and in any case my grandmother's household required much more than a household for two or three!

As soon as my mother-in-law moved to Hyde Park for the summer we moved into her house, and were promptly taken care of by her caretaker, so I still did not have to display the depths of my ignorance as a housewife.[6]

[6] Eleanor Roosevelt, *This is My Story* (New York, 1937), pp. 124-127.

FRANCES PERKINS: FDR AS NEW YORK STATE SENATOR

In his first public office, as a State Senator in the New York legislature between 1910 and 1912, FDR appeared to many of his contemporaries as the very model of an upper class, blue-blood patrician. His somewhat haughty bearing and aloof attitude made a vivid impression on Frances Perkins, as the excerpt below from her book of recollections shows. Miss Perkins was then a budding social worker, and later FDR's Secretary of Labor.

I first saw Franklin Roosevelt in 1910 at a tea dance in the house of Mrs. Walston Brown in Gramercy Park, New York City. I was studying at Columbia University for a Master's degree and working in a settlement house on a survey of the social conditions in the neighborhood.

Roosevelt had just entered politics with a Dutchess County campaign, which was not taken too seriously either by Roosevelt himself, his supporters, or his friends. The Republicans and farmers had voted for him as state senator largely because of his name. It was the era of Theodore Roosevelt, and we were all still under his spell.

Mrs. Brown was a pleasant lady who delighted to entertain serious-minded young people who were not too serious to dance and relax, strictly on tea, for such was the innocent habit of late afternoon parties of the pre-World War I period.

There was nothing particularly interesting about the tall, thin young man with the high collar and pince-nez; and I should not later have remembered this meeting except for the fact that in an interval between dances someone in the group I joined mentioned Theodore Roosevelt, speaking with some scorn of his "progressive" ideas. The tall young man named Roosevelt, I didn't catch his first name on introduction, made a spirited defense of Theodore Roosevelt, being careful to proclaim that he was not his kin except by marriage.

Like many young people, I was an ardent admirer of Theodore Roosevelt. He had been a vigorous and educative President. He had recommended to the people Jacob Riis's book *How the Other Half Lives*. I had read it, and Theodore Roosevelt's inaugural address of 1905, and had straightaway felt that the pursuit of social justice would be my vocation. Therefore this tall young man who was one of Theodore Roosevelt's admirers made a slight impression on me. We did not become well acquainted, but occasionally I saw him at purely social functions.

I did not give him a second thought until I went to Albany, as a representative of the Consumers' League, to work for passage of the fifty-four-hour bill for women, known as the Jackson-McManus bill. I had already had a conviction, a "concern," as the Quakers say, about social justice; and it was clear in my own mind that the promotion of social justice could be made to work practically. As a student and professional social worker, I was taking an active part in proposals to use the legislative authority of the state to correct social abuses—long hours, low wages, bad housing, child labor, and unsanitary conditions.

This was a period of confusion. The ancient concept of the rights of man was in conflict with the expansion and needs of big business and mass production. None of us was clear in our thinking, but our emotions were inevitably attracted by the dynamic quality of Theodore Roosevelt (whose attachment to the principles of social justice has never been sufficiently developed by his biographers) and by the qualities of leadership in social reform, both in Great Britain and in our own country, which were being demonstrated on the political plane by Lloyd George and Woodrow Wilson.

Franklin Roosevelt was then a member of the state Senate, a Democrat in an administration with a Democratic governor and a Democratic majority in both houses. No one who saw him in those years would have been likely to think of him as a potential President of the U.S.A.

I believe that at that time Franklin Roosevelt had little, if any, concern about specific social reforms. Nothing in his conversation or action would have indicated it. He was, of course, engaged in 1911 and 1912 in a violent controversy with the regular Democratic party of the state over the election by the legislature of William Sheehan as United States Senator from New York. Roosevelt and many of the Democrats of the non-professional type believed this appointment savored of "dirty politics." There can be no question but that he sincerely felt he was doing a great service in making a spectacular battle against the party organization. He won the battle, but it did not leave him with many friends in the Senate or Democratic party of the state.

I have a vivid picture of him operating on the floor of the Senate: tall and slender, very active and alert, moving around the floor, going in and out of committee rooms, rarely talking with the members, who more or less avoided him, not particularly charming (that came later), artificially serious of face, rarely smiling, with an unfortunate habit—so natural that he was unaware of it—of throwing his head up. This, combined with his pince-nez and great height, gave him the appearance of looking down his nose at most people.

It is interesting that this habit of throwing his head up, which when he was young and unchastened gave him a slightly supercilious appearance, later had a completely different effect. By 1933, and for the rest of his life, it was a gesture of courage and hope, and people were responsive to it as such.

Many staunch old Tammany Democrats in those days felt that he did look down his nose at them. I remember old Tim Sullivan, himself the acme of personal amiability, saying after a bout with Roosevelt, "Awful arrogant fellow, that Roosevelt."

I can see "that Roosevelt" now, standing back of the brass rail with two or three Democratic senators arguing with him to be "reasonable," as they called it, about something; his small mouth pursed up and slightly open, his nostrils distended, his head in the air, and his cool, remote voice saying, "No, no, I won't hear of it!"

I think he started that way not because he was born with a silver spoon in his mouth and had a good education at Harvard (which in itself constitutes a political handicap), but because he really didn't like people very much and because he had a youthful lack of humility, a streak of self-righteousness, and a deafness to the hopes, fears, and aspirations which are the common lot.

The marvel is that these handicaps were washed out of him by life, experience, punishment, and his capacity to grow. He never wholly ignored these youthful traits himself. He once said to me when he was President, "You know, I was an awfully mean cuss when I first went into politics."

During this period he was, in his personal as distinguished from his public relations, gay and agreeable. He loved to laugh in 1911 as in 1945.

The regular Democrats in Albany, however, found him austere. Personally he got great fun out of his fight against Sheehan, although it was just a drastic application of the old-fashioned reform program of honesty and intelligence in government. A young and inexperienced person like myself could not fail to observe that it *was* fun to put "corruption," as Theodore Roosevelt called it, to rout. The regular Democrats of the Tammany Hall persuasion just gritted their teeth and endured him. They disliked him, and I include among them Robert Wagner, Alfred E. Smith, Jim Foley, Harvey Ferris, Hugh Frawley, Henry Grady, and many others who thought him impossible and said so privately.

I was tremendously interested and intrigued by politicians, like Tim Sullivan of the Bowery and his cousin Christy; Senator Grady, the great orator who was nearly always slightly intoxicated when he made his orations in the Senate of New York; The MacManus [sic], called by a columnist of his day "the Devil's Deputy from Hell's Kitchen." The warm, human sympathies of these people, less than perfect as I examine their record, gave me insight into a whole stratum of American society I had not known. In contrast with these roughnecks, I don't hesitate to say now, Franklin Roosevelt seemed just an ordinary, respectable, intelligent, correct young man.

In the first Albany period of Franklin Roosevelt, I repeat, I was not much impressed by him. I knew innumerable young men who had been educated in private schools and had gone to Harvard. He did not seem different except that he had political rather than professional or scholarly interests. Many years later I realized that Franklin Roosevelt had learned from rough Tammany politicians like Tim Sullivan and the MacManus [sic]. In the spring of 1938 when I was trying to impress upon him the seriousness of a problem relating to immigration policy, he suddenly said, "Tim Sullivan used to say that the America of the future would be made out of the people who had come over in steerage and who knew in their own hearts and lives the difference between being despised and being accepted and liked." Then he added, "Poor old Tim Sullivan never understood about modern politics, but he was right about the human heart."

On the last night of the legislative session of the spring of 1912, the fifty-four-hour bill for women came to a test vote, but the forces in the New York state legislature at Albany were scattered. The Democrats had proclaimed for a number of years that they favored this law. The strategy of those of us promoting it had been to force the bill to a vote. An acceptable bill had gone through the Senate, but in the Assembly an amendment had been attached by floor vote exempting women who worked in the canneries. We had been very strongly on record as opposed to this exemption.

I later came to realize that this was part of a plan, and some of our Democratic friends by indirection had agreed to it. It was taken for granted that the friends of the bill would condemn it as amended and that it would be dropped without a roll call in the Senate. I didn't figure this out for myself. Tim Sullivan, the senator from the Bowery, told me. It was hard to believe, for I hadn't yet learned about "practical politics."

When the bill arrived in the Senate as amended, I had to decide whether to accept the amendment or see the bill die. I decided to accept the amendment and to ask to have the bill put through the Senate. Josiah Newcombe and Mayhew Wainwright, liberal Republicans, and Tim Sullivan and other Democrats really favorable to the bill advised me to do so and said they would put it through. Here the test came.

Robert Wagner, the chairman of the Rules Committee, was in the

Chair. Tim Sullivan, the next ranking member, had boarded the Hudson River boat in the belief that the bill was safe, as all had agreed to the amendment. But it was still a critical moment, as the opposition had planned not to let a vote be taken, and he had to be called back.

When Tim Sullivan came puffing up the hill after being pulled off the Albany boat, he said to me, "It's all right, me gal, we is wid ya. De bosses thought they was going to kill your bill, but they forgot about Tim Sullivan. I'm a poor man meself. Me father and me mother were poor and struggling. I seen me sister go out to work when she was only fourteen and I know we ought to help these gals by giving 'em a law which will prevent 'em from being broken down while they're still young."

This was a simple emotional response with no sophisticated political consideration involved. Certainly Tim Sullivan never realized the extent to which this type of measure twenty years later would bring nation-wide support to Franklin Roosevelt.

Tim Sullivan got the bill passed. True, it was an amended bill, but it made possible shorter hours for hundreds of thousands of women in the factories and mills of New York State.

Franklin Roosevelt did not associate himself actively with this bill, which was a measure of the progressive convictions of the politicians of 1910. I remember it clearly because I took it hard that a young man who had so much spirit did not do so well in this, which I thought a test, as did Tim Sullivan and The MacManus [sic], undoubtedly corrupt politicians.[7]

ELEANOR ROOSEVELT: POLIO

In August, 1921 FDR's rising star seemed to wane when he was struck down by polio. Below, his wife reports his illness, at first not properly diagnosed, in a letter to his half-brother, Rosy. Later, she sought to assess the impact of the illness on her husband's character and on his career.

CAMPOBELLO
August 14, 1921
Sunday

Dear Rosy,
We have had a very anxious few days as on Wed. evening Franklin

[7] Frances Perkins, *The Roosevelt I Knew* (New York: 1946), pp. 9-14.

was taken ill. It seemed a chill but Thursday he had so much pain in
his back and legs that I sent for the doctor, by Friday evening he lost
the ability to walk or move his legs but though they felt numb he can
still feel in them. Yesterday a.m. Dr. Bennett and I decided we wanted the
best opinion we could get quickly so Louis Howe (who, thank heavens,
is here, for he has been the greatest help) went with Dr. Bennett to Lubec
and they canvassed the nearby resorts and decided that the best available
diagnostician was the famous old Dr. W. W. Keen of Philadelphia and
he agreed to motor up and spend the night. He arrived about 7:30 and
made a most careful, thorough examination and the same this morning
and he thinks a clot of blood from a sudden congestion has settled in the
lower spinal cord temporarily removing the power to move though not
to feel. I have wired to New York for a masseuse as he said that was
vital and the nursing I could do, and in the meantime Louis and I are
rubbing him as well as we can. The doctor feels sure he will get well
but it may take some months. I have only told Franklin he said he could
surely go down the 15th of Sept. He did say to leave then but not before
on account of heat and to go to New York but it may have to be done
on a wheel chair. The doctor thinks absorption has already begun as he
can move his toes on one foot a little more which is very encouraging.
He has told the Dr. here just what medicines to give and what treatment to follow and we should know in the next ten days or two weeks
how things are going.

   Do you think you can meet Mama when she lands? She has asked us
to cable just before she sails and I have decided to say nothing. No letter
can reach her now and it would simply mean worry all the way home
and she will have enough once here but at least then she can do things.
I will write her a letter to quarantine saying he is ill but leave explaining
to you or if you can't meet her to Uncle Fred or whoever does meet her.
I hope you will think I am doing right and have done all I could. Of
course write me if you think of anything else. I do not want particulars
to get in the papers so I am writing the family that he is ill from the
effects of a chill and I hope will soon be better, but I shall write Uncle
Fred what I have told you and Langdon Marvin as F. cannot be at the
office to relieve him.

Affly always,

ELEANOR

My love to Betty.[8]

[8] Elliot Roosevelt, *F.D.R.: Personal Letters: 1905-1928* (New York, 1948), pp. 523-
525.

Perhaps the experience, above all others, which shaped my husband's character along more definite lines and gave him a strength and depth that he did not have as a young man was the long struggle with infantile paralysis. As he came gradually to realize that he was not going to get any better, he faced great bitterness, I am sure, though he never mentioned it. The only thing that stands out in my mind as evidence of how he suffered when he finally knew that he would never walk again was the fact that I never heard him mention golf from the day he was taken ill until the end of his life. That game epitomized to him the ability to be out of doors and to enjoy the use of his body. Though he learned to bear it, I am afraid it was always a tragedy.

He soon discovered that the way to lighten all burdens is to take them cheerfully. He regained his joy in living, his hearty laughter, his ability to be happy over little things; and though I think I was too young to realize fully at the time what a remarkable fight he was making and what a victory he had won, still everyone around him sensed a little of the struggle and helped when and as they could.

I have since come to realize and to appreciate that a strength of character was built up during these years which made him able to give complete confidence to the people of the nation when they needed it, so that when he said: "The only thing we have to fear is fear itself," they knew he held that conviction. He had lived through fear and come out successfully.[9]

WALTER LIPPMANN: FDR AS PRESIDENTIAL CANDIDATE, 1932

Despite an impressive record as Governor of New York State between 1928 and 1932 FDR's qualities of leadership were still questioned by some observers. Among those who voiced their doubts was the distinguished columnist, Walter Lippmann, who on the eve of FDR's first Presidential campaign sketched the following somewhat uncomplimentary portrait.

It is now plain that sooner or later some of Governor Roosevelt's supporters are going to feel badly let down. For it is impossible that he can continue to be such different things to such different men. He is, at the moment, the highly preferred candidate of left-wing progressives like Senator Wheeler of Montana, and of Bryan's former secretary, Repre-

[9] *Ibid.*, Foreword, pp. xviii-xix.

sentative Howard of Nebraska. He is, at the same time, receiving the enthusiastic support of the New York *Times*.

Senator Wheeler, who would like to cure the depression by debasing the currency, is Mr. Roosevelt's most conspicuous supporter in the West, and Representative Howard has this week hailed the Governor as "the most courageous enemy of the evil influences" emanating from the international bankers. The New York *Times*, on the other hand, assures its readers that "no upsetting plans, no Socialistic proposals, however mild and winning in form," could appeal to the Governor.

The Roosevelt bandwagon would seem to be moving in two opposite directions.

There are two questions raised by this curious situation. The first is why Senator Wheeler and the *Times* should have such contradictory impressions of the common candidate. The second, which is also the more important question, is which has guessed rightly.

The art of carrying water on both shoulders is highly developed in American politics, and Mr. Roosevelt has learned it. His message to the Legislature, or at least that part of it devoted to his Presidential candidacy, is an almost perfect specimen of the balanced antithesis. Thus at one place we learn that the public demands "plans for the reconstruction of a better ordered civilization" and in another place that "the American system of economics and government is everlasting." The first sentence is meant for Senator Wheeler and the second for the New York *Times*.

The message is so constructed that a left-wing progressive can read it and find just enough of his own phrases in it to satisfy himself that Franklin D. Roosevelt's heart is in the right place. He will find an echo of Governor La Follette's recent remarks about the loss of "economic liberty." He will find an echo of Governor La Follette's impressive discussion about the increasing concentration of wealth and how it does not guarantee an intelligent or a fair use of that wealth. He will find references to "plans." On the other hand, there are all necessary assurances to the conservatives. "We should not seek in any way to destroy or to tear down"; our system is "everlasting"; we must insist "on the permanence of our fundamental institutions."

That this is a studied attempt to straddle the whole country I have no doubt whatever. Every newspaper man knows the whole bag of tricks by heart. He knows too that the practical politician supplements these two-faced platitudes by what are called private assurances, in which he tells his different supporters what he knows they would like to hear. Then, when they read the balanced antithesis, each believes the half that he has been reassured about privately and dismisses the rest as not significant. That, ladies and gentlemen, is how the rabbit comes out of the hat, that is how it is possible to persuade Senator Wheeler and the New York *Times* that you are their man.

In the case of Mr. Roosevelt, it is not easy to say with certainty whether his left-wing or his right-wing supporters are the more deceived. The reason is that Franklin D. Roosevelt is a highly impressionable person, without a firm grasp of public affairs and without very strong convictions. He might plump for something which would shock the conservatives. There is no telling. Yet when Representative Howard of Nebraska says that he is "the most dangerous enemy of evil influences," New Yorkers who know the Governor know that Mr. Howard does not know the Governor. For Franklin D. Roosevelt is an amiable man with many philanthropic impulses, but he is not the dangerous enemy of anything. He is too eager to please. The notion, which seems to prevail in the West and South, that Wall Street fears him, is preposterous. Wall Street thinks he is too dry, not that he is too radical. Wall Street does not like some of his supporters. Wall Street does not like his vagueness, and the uncertainty as to what he does think, but if any Western Progressive thinks that the Governor has challenged directly or indirectly the wealth concentrated in New York City, he is mightily mistaken.

Mr. Roosevelt is, as a matter of fact, an excessively cautious politician. He has been Governor for three years, and I doubt whether anyone can point to a single act of his which involved any political risk. Certainly his water power policy has cost him nothing, for the old interests who fought Smith have been displaced by more enlightened capitalists quite content to let the state finance the development. I can think of nothing else that could be described as evidence of his willingness to attack vested interests, and I can think of one outstanding case in which he has shown the utmost reluctance to attack them. I refer to his relations with Tammany.

It is well known in New York, though apparently not in the West, that Governor Roosevelt had to be forced into assisting the exposure of corruption in New York City. It is well known in New York that, through his patronage, he has supported the present powers in Tammany Hall. It is well known that his policy has been to offend Tammany just as little as he dared in the face of the fact that an investigation of Tammany had finally to be undertaken. It is true that he is not popular in Tammany Hall, but, though they do not like him, they vote for him. For there is a working arrangement between him and Tammany. That was proved last November when the Tammany organization went to the polls for the amendment which Smith opposed and Roosevelt sponsored. Tammany had no interest in that amendment. It dealt with reforestation hundreds of miles from the sidewalks of New York. Yet it was the Tammany machine which gave the Governor his victory.

I do not say that Mr. Roosevelt might not at some time in the next few months fight Tammany. I do say that on his record these last three years he will fight Tammany only if and when he decides it is safe and profitable to do so. For Franklin D. Roosevelt is no crusader. He is no tribune of the people. He is no enemy of entrenched privilege. He is a pleasant man who, without any important qualifications for the office, would very much like to be President.

It is meaningless for him to talk about "leadership practical, sound, courageous and alert." He has been Governor in the community which has been the financial center of the world during the last year of the boom and the two years of the depression. The Governor of New York is listened to when he speaks. Can anyone point to anything Mr. Roosevelt has said or done in those three years to provide the leadership we should all so much like to have had? I do not think anyone can. He has carefully refrained during these years from exerting any kind of leadership on any national question which was controversial. That was probably shrewd politics. It has helped his candidacy. But as a result of his strategic silence nobody knows where he stands on any of the great questions which require practical, sound, courageous and alert leadership.[10]

[10] Walter Lippmann, *Interpretations, 1931-1932* (New York, 1933), pp. 259-263.

4
FDR Viewed as President

What were FDR's motives as President? Contemporary observers differed widely in their assessment of the role which he sought to fill in carrying out his objectives. This was true of domestic as well as of foreign policies. Miss Frances Perkins, Secretary of Labor in FDR's Cabinet, emphasized his pragmatic attitude. Another perspective was provided by Sam Rosenman, one of FDR's major speech writers. Rosenman considered the President as filling a symbolic role, as a restorer of confidence. This psychological function FDR accomplished by means of his skillful use of the mass media, especially the radio. Henry Morgenthau, Jr., on the other hand, revealed some of the frustrations often felt by FDR's associates when their chief chose to play the role of improvisor. Critics of the New Deal were much harsher. Herbert Hoover called FDR a dictator. Al Smith charged him with undermining the Constitution. Father Charles E. Coughlin damned him as a tool of financial power. Earl Browder and the Communists considered him an exploiter of the working class. And in the realm of diplomacy, FDR was no less controversial. If Adolph Hitler charged him with having instigated World War II, Secretary of War Henry L. Stimson found him to be an effective war leader. Off the record, Premier Joseph Stalin distrusted FDR, while Winston Churchill eulogized him as a great world leader. As if to confound his contemporaries, FDR rarely revealed the whole range of his motives to anyone. Instead, he kept all of them guessing, friendly co-workers as well as hostile critics. Indeed, this was the essence of the "Roosevelt Style" during his twelve years in office.

FRANCES PERKINS: FDR, PRAGMATIST

An astute appraisal of FDR's political and economic beliefs was made by Frances Perkins, who, as Secretary of Labor in FDR's Cabinet, was in frequent and close personal contact with her chief. In attempting to explain FDR she stressed his moralism, his simplicity, and his humanity. But above all, she felt that an important key to

*understanding FDR was his pragmatic approach, his willingness to
experiment.*

I knew Roosevelt long enough and under enough circumstances to
be quite sure that he was no political or economic radical. I take it that
the essence of economic radicalism is to believe that the best system is
the one in which private ownership of the means of production is abolished in favor of public ownership. But Roosevelt took the status quo
in our economic system as much for granted as his family. They were
part of his life, and so was our system; he was content with it. He felt
that it ought to be humane, fair, and honest, and that adjustments ought
to be made so that the people would not suffer from poverty and neglect,
and so that all would share.

He thought business could be a fine art and could be conducted on
moral principles. He thought the test ought to be whether or not business
is conducted partly for the welfare of the community. He could not accept the idea that the sole purpose of business was to make more and
more money. He thought business should make and distribute goods with
enough profit to give the owners a comfortable living and enable them
to save something to invest in other productive enterprises. Yes, he felt
that stockholders had a place and right and that a business ought to be
conducted so that they would earn modest interest, while the workers got
good wages and the community profited by low prices and steady work.

But he couldn't see why a man making enough money should want to
go on scheming and plotting, sacrificing and living under nervous tension, just to make more money. That, of course, made him unable to
sympathize with the ambitions and drive of much of the American business fraternity. But he liked and got along well with those businessmen
who shared, as many did, the point of view that business is conducted
partly for the welfare of the country as well as to make money. They
liked and trusted him and understood his objectives. Gerard Swope of
the General Electric Company, Thomas J. Watson of the International
Business Machines Company, Ernest Draper of the Hills Brothers Company, Donald and Hugh Comer, southern textile manufacturers, who
had a humane if not a trade union conception of the rights of their
workers and of the employers' duty in relation to them, were all com-
prehensible to the President. He liked Walter Chrysler, although I am
not sure that Chrysler fully embraced the idea that enough is enough,
particularly if his rivals were making more. But he did have some of the
attitude that there was nothing remarkable in itself about making money.

It is true that Roosevelt never met a payroll, and many businessmen took it into their heads that he could not possibly comprehend business unless he had had that experience. This, of course, is part of the limitation of the business fraternity itself.

Roosevelt was entirely willing to try experiments. He had no theoretical or ideological objections to public ownership when that was necessary, but it was his belief that it would greatly complicate the administrative system if we had too much. He recognized, however, that certain enterprises could best be carried on under public control. He recognized that we probably would never have enough cheap electric power to supply the needs of the people if the Government did not undertake vast programs in the Tennessee and Missouri valleys, and he believed that plenty of power at low rates was necessary for the development of a high standard of living and for business progress. Just as the need for production in wartime is so great that the government must take a hand in it, so he was able to accept the idea that in peacetime too the Government must sometimes carry on enterprises because of the enormous amount of capital expenditure required or the preponderance of the experimental element. He was willing to concede that there were some fields in which such Government participation might be required permanently. But he always resisted the frequent suggestion of the Government's taking over railroads, mines, etc., on the ground that it was unnecessary and would be a clumsy way to get the service needed.

A superficial young reporter once said to Roosevelt in my presence, "Mr. President, are you a Communist?"

"No."

"Are you a capitalist?"

"No."

"Are you a Socialist?"

"No," he said, with a look of surprise as if he were wondering what he was being cross examined about.

The young man said, "Well, what is your philosophy then?"

"Philosophy?" asked the President, puzzled. "Philosophy? I am a Christian and a Democrat—that's all."

Those two words expressed, I think, just about what he was. They expressed the extent of his political and economic radicalism. He was willing to do experimentally whatever was necessary to promote the Golden Rule and other ideals he considered to be Christian, and whatever could be done under the Constitution of the United States and under the principles which have guided the Democratic party.[1]

[1] Frances Perkins, *The Roosevelt I Knew* (New York, 1946), pp. 328-333.

HENRY MORGENTHAU, JR.: FDR, IMPROVISOR

Even some of FDR's close associates such as his Secretary of the
Treasury, Henry Morgenthau, Jr., sometimes shrank from the Presi-
dent's seeming irresponsibility in making important policy decisions.
A prime example was the manner in which FDR chose to fight the
economic recession of 1937. In his later reminiscences Morgenthau
related how appalled he was when FDR, without consulting him,
decided early in 1938 to commence large scale federal spending. The
doubts Morgenthau recorded in the following excerpts were typical
of the uneasiness which many of FDR's advisors shared about their
chief's impending actions or decisions. The President, on the other
hand, immensely enjoyed keeping his subordinates guessing, and in
a continual state of suspense.

The Secretary feared that the Administration was drifting. Not just
unemployment but all evidence on business conditions alarmed him. On
February 1 the Treasury's Research Division reported that the woolen
industry was in unusually bad shape, automobile production was off,
steel production had turned down, and there had been another sharp
drop in construction. Morgenthau could only say: "Gosh!" He had never
felt lower.

Nor had his fiscal policies ever been under sharper attack. The advocates of countercyclical spending received timely support from their intellectual mentor, John Maynard Keynes, who on February 1, 1938, wrote
Roosevelt an unsolicited letter about the recession. The key to recovery,
Keynes maintained, was spending. Easy short-term money and the creation of an adequate system of relief, important though they were, could
not and would not in themselves suffice. Recovery depended upon large-
scale recourse to public works and other investments in capital goods
guaranteed by the government. The Administration, he suggested, was
especially subject to criticism for its "wicked" handling of the housing
problem. Housing was by far the most important aid to recovery because of the large and continuing scale of potential demand, its wide
geographical distribution, and the relative independence of housing
finance from the stock exchanges. Keynes therefore advised putting "most
of the eggs in the housing basket," and making absolutely sure that they
were hatched without delay, if necessary through the use of direct subsidies.

He also criticized the deadlock on utilities. A good deal of what was alleged about the "wickedness" of the utility holding companies, he said, was surely "wide of the mark." "The real criminals" had cleared out long ago. Personally he thought there was a great deal to be said for the ownership of all of the utilities by the government, but if public opinion was not yet ripe for this, he saw no object "in chasing utilities around the lot every other week." He considered it wise instead to "make peace on liberal terms," guaranteeing fair earnings on new investment and a fair basis of evaluation in the event of future government purchase. He spoke, too, of the railroads as potential sources of substantial demand for new capital expenditures. Nationalize them, he wrote, if the time was "ripe"; if not, "take pity" on the overwhelming problems of their management, and "let the dead bury their dead." "To an Englishman," Keynes said, "you Americans, like the Irish, are so terribly historically-minded!"

The recession, Keynes continued, was also in part psychological in origin. For this he blamed the President's attitude toward businessmen. "Businessmen," Keynes proposed, "have a different set of delusions from politicians; and need, therefore, different handling. They are, however, much milder than politicians, at the same time allured and terrified by the glare of publicity, easily persuaded to be 'patriots,' perplexed, bemused, indeed terrified, yet only too anxious to take a cheerful view, vain perhaps but very unsure of themselves, pathetically responsive to a kind word. You could do anything you liked with them, if you would treat them (even the big ones), not as wolves and tigers, but as domestic animals by nature, even though they have been badly brought up and not trained as you would wish. It is a mistake to think that they are more *immoral* than politicians. If you work them into the surly, obstinate, terrified mood, of which domestic animals, wrongly handled, are so capable, the nation's burdens will not get carried to market; and in the end public opinion will veer their way."

Morgenthau read Keynes's letter with special interest, for Roosevelt instructed him to answer it. The task was agreeable. It gave the Secretary the chance to speak for the Administration, and by a calculated silence to reject advice he disliked. He was deliberately noncommittal. "It was very pleasant and encouraging to know," he wrote, "that you are in agreement with so much of the Administration's economic program. This confirmation coming from so eminent an economist is indeed welcome. Your analysis . . . is very interesting. The emphasis you put upon . . . housing . . . is well placed."

The emphasis Keynes put upon government spending Morgenthau simply ignored. He had long since registered his disagreement. But private investment concerned him deeply, and he had begun, long before he wrote, to investigate ways to stimulate it. Like Keynes, he felt that businessmen needed reassurance, but, with Roosevelt, he questioned their benevolence. He had large sympathy for small businesses but little for some big ones. He wanted to help the utilities, but he also felt that they had to be shown how to behave. He considered housing vital, but he doubted the wisdom of direct federal expenditures for construction. He believed, as he long had, that easy money would invite private investment and that business confidence would ensure it. Allowing always for relief, he considered economy in government the surest source of that confidence. So he had believed when he addressed the Academy of Political Science in November; so he believed when he addressed Keynes three months later.

Roosevelt, accepting Morgenthau's noncommittal reply for his own signature, could have had no doubt about what it implied. Morgenthau therefore felt that he still had an opportunity to conquer the recession without capitulating to the spenders. With the President apparently still undecided about what medicine he would prescribe, the Secretary in February and March recommended a number of remedies which were intended, in one way or another, to force or to induce a degree of private spending that would make a Keynesian policy unnecessary and undesirable. Keynes and his disciples, Morgenthau insisted, had a set of delusions all of their own.[2]

On March 25, while Roosevelt was on vacation at Warm Springs, the stock market had taken another sickening dip. This, as Morgenthau later observed, was the signal for new activity on the part of the spenders. Harry Hopkins, armed with memoranda from Leon Henderson and Aubrey Williams, camped on the President's doorstep. Before Roosevelt left Georgia, he decided he had to spend his way to recovery.

Morgenthau received his first intimation of the change on April 4 when Wallace telephoned him at Sea Island. The President, Wallace said, was "rarin' to go." He had instructed Wallace and Jones to work out a program for housing, flood control, rural rehabilitation, and loans to industry. He was also planning, Morgenthau learned two days later, additional appropriations for the Civilian Conservation Corps and the Works Progress Administration.

Under Secretary Roswell Magill, who attended the Cabinet meeting of April 5 in Morgenthau's place, gave the Secretary a full account of Roosevelt's state of mind. Congressional leaders, the President had complained, were thinking of going home after passing bills on the Navy, taxes, and

[2] John M. Blum, ed., *From the Morgenthau Diaries* (Boston, 1959), pp. 402-404.

government reorganization. This would be fiddling while Rome burned, he said. He had done a lot of reading at Warm Springs, and he had reports from all branches of the government. The situation was bad not only for the country but also for the Democratic party, which might lose the fall election if conditions continued as they were.

The requests for funds he had already made, Roosevelt said, would at best maintain the existing state of affairs without making possible any improvement. These requests included $1 billion 250 million for relief for the first seven months of the fiscal year 1939, $50 million to keep three hundred CCC camps going, and $300 or $400 million for the RFC. He was now thinking about what additional action to take. He contemplated at least lowering reserve requirements, desterilizing more gold, and amending the housing law so that construction could begin before localities contributed the 10 per cent required of them.

Farley recommended expanding the post office building program, but the President said that money for post offices would go mainly to country towns, where unemployment was less severe than in the cities.

Garner thought the national debt was already enormous and wondered whether the country could stand any more. He also believed that the government had to move more people out of the cities into rural areas. As between the success of the Democratic party and the success of the country, the patriotic Vice President declared for the country.

Roosevelt said he was for the country, too, but that if the Democrats were defeated in the fall, a third party might arise and the Republicans win the election of 1940. That would mean the ruin of many New Deal reforms. He wanted to spend money, he explained, in such a way as to bring it back to the Treasury ultimately; what he needed was suggestions for how to do so. He also wanted the Treasury to give him full information on reserve requirements and desterilization.

Treasury officials elected to comment on Roosevelt's whole program. On April 7 Dan Bell wrote that the recession would reduce revenues for 1939 by at least $519 million. On account of the recession, furthermore, the President had already decided to request emergency expenditures above the estimate of the previous fall by some $2.1 billion. Bell foresaw a net deficit of at least $2.719 billion, of which only a small fraction could be offset by desterilizing gold or using deposits in the unemployment insurance trust fund.

In a memorandum on April 8, the Research Division questioned the wisdom of spending for public works, which would create anxiety within the business community. Instead the memorandum recommended three moves to increase business confidence and private spending: liberal relief appropriations, desterilization of the gold remaining in the inactive fund, and restoration of reserve requirements to the level existing before the Board of Governors first raised them.

Morgenthau was less cautious than his subordinates. Knowing Roosevelt as he did, he realized he had to meet him part way. On the train from Sea Island to Washington he wrote a carefully calculated "Memorandum for the President," which he intended to deliver as soon as he arrived on the evening of Sunday, April 10. The time was propitious, Morgenthau began, for Roosevelt to present to the people a comprehensive statement of policy. He should state first his long-run objectives and describe the major legislation needed during the coming two years to attain them. That legislation should include the creation of some kind of transportation authority, appropriations for the investigation and prosecution of monopolies, a wage and hour law, and the taxation of tax-exempt bonds. Second, the program should consist of an outline of specific steps, administrative as well as legislative, which Roosevelt proposed to take in order to eliminate inefficiencies and failures in parts of the New Deal already under way. Third, Morgenthau suggested the President prepare a comprehensive government spending and lending program, coupled with measures to stimulate private re-employment. It was most important, the Secretary wrote, to put to work immediately the ten million or more unemployed. But that did not excuse waste. In formulating a program, the Administration would have to correlate expenditures with the geographical distribution of unemployment.

Obviously the recession had destroyed Morgenthau's hopes for balancing the budget in 1939. But he still favored minimizing the total deficit, relying insofar as possible on lending rather than spending, concentrating spending insofar as possible on relief and work relief rather than on large-scale public works, and making the lending and relief policies handmaidens of a central purpose to spur private investment.

Roosevelt, however, had come to quite different conclusions. On the night of April 10, Morgenthau had a long and unhappy talk at the White House with the President, Hopkins, and Jimmy Roosevelt.

"We have been traveling fast this last week and have covered a lot of ground," the President said, "and you will have to hurry to catch up."

"Mr. President," Morgenthau said, "maybe I never can catch up."

Roosevelt smiled. "Oh, yes, you can—in a couple of hours."

With that he presented his ideas. Morgenthau's heart sank. It was clear that Hopkins had "sold" the President on spending. Ickes was to be put back into the business of lending money to states and municipalities. The

United States Housing Authority was to have its loan authorizations doubled. The Federal Housing Administration was to build $500 million worth of houses. A transcontinental highway was to be started. And so on. Morgenthau listened and then read his own memorandum, with its emphasis on private re-employment.

When he finished, the President asked, "You are in agreement with this?"

"What you have outlined not only frightens me but will frighten the country," Morgenthau replied. "How much is it going to cost?"

"Oh," Roosevelt said, "we have all of that . . . we have all that."

Morgenthau asked to see a list of proposed expenditures, but none was forthcoming. "Please, Mr. President," he said on departing, "don't decide on this until you sleep on it."

The Secretary arrived at the Treasury the next morning depressed and angry. "I don't mind telling you gentlemen what I heard last night," he said to his staff. "The way it was put up to me last night just scared me to death—worse than I've been scared—and the thing hasn't been thought through. And fear begets fear—I mean . . . the President's attitude . . . in 1933, was, let's be calm and do things and overcome fear, but fear begets fear. . . . They had a conference—lasted an hour before I came —in advance of my coming—and I think the whole thing is finished, and there hasn't been a single person in the Treasury that knows a single thing about this. . . . I'm awfully afraid that the cards are all stacked against us."

The new program, Morgenthau went on, would wreck the RFC before Jones had a chance to get started. If Ickes and Hopkins as well as Jones were lending to municipalities, there would be an awful mess. The spenders had carried the day and the President, too. "They have just stampeded him during the week I was away. He was completely stampeded. They stampeded him like cattle." [3]

HERBERT HOOVER: FDR, DICTATOR

To Herbert Hoover, FDR's New Deal heralded the end of individual liberties and democratic government in America. Hoover believed that his successor harbored authoritarian tendencies comparable to those of Hitler in Germany and Mussolini in Italy. As he travelled through the nation in an effort to rally opposition to the New Deal, Hoover forcefully presented his impression of FDR and warned Americans to beware of his programs. Below are ex-

[3] *Ibid.,* pp. 417-421.

cerpts from Hoover's speeches which emphasize the dangers of FDR's radicalism.

In Central Europe the march of Socialist or Fascist dictatorships and their destruction of liberty did not set out with guns and armies. Dictators began their ascent to the seats of power through the elections provided by liberal institutions. Their weapons were promise and hate. They offered the mirage of Utopia to those in distress. They flung the poison of class hatred. They may not have maimed the bodies of men but they maimed their souls.

The 1932 campaign was a pretty good imitation of this first stage of European tactics. You may recall the promises of the abundant life, the propaganda of hate.

Once seated in office the first demand of these European despotisms was for power and "action." Legislatures were told they "must" delegate their authorities. Their free debate was suppressed. The powers demanded are always the same pattern. They all adopted Planned Economy. They regimented industry and agriculture. They put the government into business. They engaged in gigantic government expenditures. They created vast organizations of spoils henchmen and subsidized dependents. They corrupted currency and credit. They drugged the thinking of the people with propaganda at the people's expense.

If there are any items in this stage in the march of European collectivism that the New Deal has not imitated it must have been an oversight.

But at this point this parallel with Europe halts—at least for the present. The American people should thank Almighty God for the Constitution and the Supreme Court. They should be grateful to a courageous press.

You might contemplate what would have happened if Mr. Roosevelt could have appointed enough Supreme Court Justices in the first year of his Administration. Suppose these New Deal acts had remained upon the statute books. We would have been a regimented people. Have you any assurance that he will not have the appointments if he is re-elected?

The succeeding stages of violence and outrage by which European despotisms have crushed all liberalism and all freedom have filled our headlines for years.

But what comes next in the United States? Have the New Dealers dropped their ideas of centralization of government? Have they abandoned the notion of regimenting the people into a Planned Economy?

Has that greed for power become cooled by the resistance of a people with a heritage of freedom? Will they resume if they are re-elected?

When we examine the speeches of Tugwell, Wallace, Ickes and others, we see little indications of repentance.

Let me say this: America is no monarchy where the Chief of State is not responsible for his ministers. It has been traditional in our government since the beginning that the important officials appointed by the President speak in tune with his mind. That is imperative if there is to be intellectual honesty in government. President Roosevelt finds no difficulty in disciplining his officials. Witness the prompt dismissal of those who did not publicly agree with him. The President will not discharge these men on whom his New Deal is dependent. No matter what the new platform of the New Deal party may say, the philosophy of collectivism and that greed for power are in the blood of some part of these men. Do you believe that if re-elected they intend to stand still among the wreckage of their dreams? In the words of Mr. Hopkins, perhaps we are too profanely dumb to understand.[4]

*　　*　　*

Through four years of experience this New Deal attack upon free institutions has emerged as the transcendent issue in America.

All the men who are seeking for mastery in the world today are using the same weapons. They sing the same songs. They all promise the joys of Elysium without effort. But their philosophy is founded on the coercion and compulsory organization of men. True liberal government is founded on the emancipation of men. This is the issue upon which men are imprisoned and dying in Europe right now.

The rise of this issue has dissolved our old party lines. The New Deal repudiation of Democracy has left the Republican party alone the guardian of the Ark of the Covenant with its charter of freedom. The tremendous import of this issue, the peril to our country has brought the support of the ablest leaders of the Democratic party. It is no passing matter which enlists side by side the fighting men who have opposed each other over many years. It is the unity demanded by a grave danger to the Republic. Their sacrifice to join with us has no parallel in American history since the Civil War. There run through my mind great words from the Battle Hymn of the Republic:

> . . . "in the watchfires of a hundred circling camps
> They have builded them an altar" . . .

[4] *The New York Times,* June 11, 1936.

I realize that this danger of centralized personal government disturbs only thinking men and women. But surely the NRA and the AAA alone, should prove what the New Deal philosophy of government means even to those who don't think.

In these instances the Supreme Court, true to their oaths to support the Constitution, saved us temporarily. But Congress in obedience to their oaths should never have passed on these acts. The President should never have signed them. But far more important than that, if these men were devoted to the American system of liberty they never would have proposed acts based on the coercion and compulsory organization of men.

Freedom does not die from frontal attack. It dies because men in power no longer believe in a system based upon Liberty.

Mr. Roosevelt on this eve of election has started using the phrases of freedom. He talks sweetly of personal liberty, of individualism, of the American system, of the profit system. He says now that he thinks well of capitalism, and individual enterprise. His devotion to private property seems to be increasing. He has suddenly found some good economic royalists. And he is a staunch supporter of the Constitution. Two days ago he rededicated the Statue of Liberty in New York. She has been the forgotten woman.

Four years ago we also heard many phrases which turned out not to mean what they were thought to have meant. In order that we may be sure this time will Mr. Roosevelt reply in plain words:

Does he propose to revive the nine acts which the Supreme Court has rejected as invasions of the safeguards of free men?

Has he abandoned his implied determination to change the Constitution? Why not tell the American people before election what changes he proposes? Does he intend to stuff the Court itself? Why does the New Deal not really lay its cards on the table?

But their illegal invasions of the Constitution are but the minor artillery with which this New Deal philosophy of government is being forced upon us. They are now using a more subtle and far more effective method of substituting personal power and centralized government for the institutions of free men. It is not by violation of the Constitution that they are making headway today. It is through taking vast sums of the people's money and then manipulating its spending to build up personal power. By this route relief has been centralized in their hands. By this route government has entered into business in competition with the citizen. In his way a score of new instruments of public power have been created. By this route the ordinary functions of government have been uselessly expanded with a double bookkeeping to conceal it. Public funds are used right and left to subsidize special groups of our citizens and special regions of the country. At public expense there is a steady drip of propaganda to poison the public mind.

Through this spending there grows a huge number of citizens with a selfish vested interest in continuing this centralization of power. It has also made millions of citizens dependent upon the government.

Thus also have been built huge political bureaucracies hungry for more power. This use of money has enabled the independence of members of Congress to be sapped by the pork barrel. It has subtly undermined the rights and the responsibility of States and local governments. Out of all this we see government daily by executive orders instead of by open laws openly arrived at.

The New Deal taxes are in forms which stifle the growth of small business and discourage new enterprise. By stifling private enterprise the field is tilled for further extension of government enterprise. Intricate taxes are interpreted by political bureaucrats who coerce and threaten our business men. By politically managed currency the President has seized the power to alter all wages, all prices, all debts, all savings at will. But that is not the worst. They are creating personal power over votes. That crushes the first safeguard of liberty.

Does Mr. Roosevelt not admit all this in his last report on the state of the Union: "We have built up new instruments of public power" which he admits could "provide shackles for the liberties of the people." Does freedom permit any man or any government any such power? Have the people ever voted for these shackles?

Has he abandoned this "new order," this "planned economy" that he has so often talked about? Will he discharge these associates of his who daily preached the "new order" but whom he does not now allow to appear in this campaign?

Is Mr. Roosevelt not asking for a vote of confidence on these very breaches of liberty?

Is not this very increase in personal power the suicide road upon which every democratic government has died from the time of Greece and Rome down to the dozen liberal governments that have perished in Europe during this past twenty years? [5]

ALFRED E. SMITH: FDR, DESTROYER OF THE CONSTITUTION

Some of the most bitter barbs were aimed at FDR by a few of his erstwhile supporters, of whom former Governor Al Smith was

[5] *The New York Times,* October 31, 1936.

prominent. Dismayed by FDR's conduct in the Presidency, by 1935 Smith was accusing his former protegé of undermining the Constitution and usurping legislative powers. So strong was Smith's repugnance that he refused to support FDR for a second term, and openly rejected the New Deal in its entirety. In a speech below, delivered to the American Liberty League—composed of wealthy businessmen opposed to FDR—Smith explained some of the reasons for his disenchantment.

Mr. Chairman, members and guests of the American Liberty League, and my friends listening in, as I have been told by the newspapers from all parts of the United States:

At the outset of my remarks let me make one thing perfectly clear. I am not a candidate for any nomination by any party, at any time. What is more, I do not intend even to lift my right hand to secure any nomination from any party at any time.

Further than that, I have no axe to grind. There is nothing personal in this whole performance in so far as I am concerned. I have no feeling against any man, woman or child in the United States. I am in possession of supreme happiness and comfort. I represent no group, no man, and I speak for no man or no group, but I do speak for what I believe to be the best interests of the great rank and file of the American people in which class I belong.

Now, I am here tonight also because I have a great love for the United States of America. I love it for what I know it has meant to mankind since the day of its institution. I love it because I feel that it has grown to be a great stabilizing force in world civilization. I love it, above everything else, for the opportunity that it offers to every man and every woman that desires to take advantage of it.

No man that I know or that I probably ever read of has any more reason to love it than I have. They kept the gateway open for me. It is a matter of common knowledge throughout the country, and I do not state it boastfully, because it is well known, that deprived by poverty in my early years of an education, that gateway showed me how it was possible to go from a newsboy on the sidewalks of New York to the Governorship of the greatest State in the Union.

Just get the platform of the Democratic party and get the platform of the Socialist party and lay them down on your dining-room table, side by side, and get a heavy lead pencil and scratch out the word "Democratic" and scratch out the word "Socialist," and let the two platforms lay there, and then study the record of the present administration up to date.

After you have done that, make your mind up to pick up the platform that more nearly squares with the record, and you will have your hand on the Socialist platform; you would not dare touch the Democratic platform.

And incidentally, let me say that it is not the first time in recorded history that a group of men have stolen the livery of the church to do the work of the devil.

If you study this whole situation you will find that is at the bottom of all our troubles. This country was organized on the principles of a representative democracy, and you can't mix socialism or communism with that. They are like oil and water. They are just like oil and water, they refuse to mix.

Incidentally, let me say to you that is the reason why the United States Supreme Court is working overtime, throwing the alphabet out of the window, three letters at a time.

I am going to let you in on something else. How do you suppose all this happened? This is the way it happened. The young brain trusters caught the Socialists in swimming and they ran away with their clothes.

Now, it is all right with me, it is all right with me, if they want to disguise themselves as Karl Marx or Lenin or any of the rest of that bunch, but I won't stand for their allowing them to march under the banner of Jackson or Cleveland.

Now, what is worrying me is: Where does that leave us millions of Democrats? My mind is all fixed upon the convention in June in Philadelphia. The committee on resolutions is about to report. The preamble to the platform is:

"We, the representatives of the Democratic party, in convention assembled, heartily endorse the Democratic administration."

What happened to the recital of Jefferson and Jackson and Cleveland when that resolution was read out? Why, for us it is a washout. There is only one of two things we can do, we can either take on the mantle of hypocrisy or we can take a walk, and we will probably do the latter.

Now, leave the platform alone for a little while. What about this attack that has been made upon the fundamental institutions of this country, who threatens them, and did we have any warning of this threat? Why, you don't have to study party platforms, you don't have to read books, you don't have to listen to professors of economics. You will find the whole thing incorporated in the greatest declaration of political principle that ever came from the hand of man—the Declaration of Independence and the Constitution of the United States.

Always have in your mind that the Constitution and the first ten amendments were drafted by refugees and by sons of refugees, by men with bitter memories of European oppression and hardship, by men who brought to this country and handed down to their descendants an abiding fear of arbitrary, centralized government and autocracy and—listen— all the bitterness and all the hatred of the Old World was distilled, in our Constitution, into the purest democracy that the world has ever known.

There are just three principles, and in the interest of brevity I will read them. I can read them quicker than talk them.

First, a Federal Government strictly limited in its powers, with all other powers except those expressly mentioned reserved to the States and to the people, so as to insure States' rights, guarantee home rule and preserve freedom of individual initiative and local control.

That is simple enough. The difference between the State Constitution and the Federal Constitution is that in the State you can do anything you want to do provided it is not prohibited by the Constitution, but in the Federal Government, according to that document, you can do only that which that Constitution tells you that you can do.

What is the trouble? Congress has overstepped its power, it has gone beyond that constitutional limitation, and it has enacted laws that not only violate that, but violate the home rule and the States' rights principle. And who says that?

Did I say it? Not at all. That was said by the United States Supreme Court in the last ten or twelve days.

Second, the government with three independent branches, Congress to make the laws, the Executives to execute them, the Supreme Court, and so forth, and you all know that.

In the name of heaven, where is the independence of Congress? Why, they just laid right down. They are flatter on the Congressional floor than the rug under this table here.

They centered all their powers in the Executives, and that is the reason why you read in the newspapers reference to Congress as the rubber-stamp Congress.

We all know that the most important bills were drafted by the brain trusters and sent over to Congress and passed by Congress without consideration, without debate, and, without meaning any offense at all to my Democratic brethren in Congress, I think I can safely say without

90 per cent of them knowing what was in the bills, what was the meaning of the list that came over, and beside certain items was "must."

Speaking for the rank and file of the American people, we don't want any Executive to tell Congress what it must do. We don't want any Congress to tell the Executive what he must do.

We don't want Congress or the Executive, jointly or severally, to tell the United States Supreme Court what it must do.

On the other hand, we don't want the United States Supreme Court to tell either of them what they must do. What we want, and what we insist upon, and what we are going to have, is the absolute preservation of this balance of power which is the keystone upon which the whole theory of democratic government has got to rest, and when you rattle it you rattle the whole structure.

Of course, when our forefathers wrote the Constitution, it couldn't be possible that they had in their minds that that was going to be all right for all time to come, so they said, "No, we will provide a manner and method of amending," and that is set forth in the document itself. And during our national life we amended it many times.

We amended it once by mistake, and we corrected it.

And what did we do? We took the amendment out. Fine! That is the way we ought to do it. By recourse to the people.

But we don't want an administration that takes a shot at it in the dark and that ducks away from it and dodges away from it and tries to put something over in contradiction of it upon any theory that there is going to be a great public power in favor of it and it is possible that the United States Supreme Court may be intimidated into a friendly opinion with respect to it.

But I found all during my public life that Almighty God built this country and He did not give us that kind of a Supreme Court.

Now, this is pretty tough for me to have to go after my own party this way, but I submit that there is a limit to blind loyalty.

As a young man in the Democratic party I witnessed the rise and fall of Bryan and Bryanism, and in the memory of Bryan, what he did to our party, I know how long it took to build it after he got finished with it. But let me say this, for the everlasting memory of Bryan and the men that followed him, that they had the energy and the courage and the honesty to put into the platform just what their leaders told them.

They put the American people in the position of making an intelligent choice when they went to the polls. The fact of this whole thing is, I speak now not only of the executive but of the Legislature at the same time—that they promised one set of things. They repudiated that promise, and they launched off on a program of action totally different.

Well, in twenty-five years of experience I have known both parties to fail to carry out some of the planks of their platform, but this is the first time that I have known a party, upon such a huge scale, not only not to carry out the planks, but to do directly the opposite thing to what they promised.

Now, suggestions—and I make these as a Democrat, acting for the success of my party, and I make them in good faith. Here are my suggestions:

Number 1—I suggest for the members of my party on Capitol Hill here in Washington that they take their minds off the Tuesday that follows the first Monday in November.

Just take your mind off it to the end that you may do the right thing and not the expedient thing.

Yes, I suggest to them that they dig up the 1932 platform from the grave that they buried it in and read it over and study it, read life into it and follow it in legislative and executive action to the end that they make good their promises to the American people when they put forth that platform and the candidate that stood upon it 100 per cent—in short, make good.

Third, I would suggest that they stop compromising with the fundamental principles laid down by Jackson and Jefferson and Cleveland.

Fourth, stop attacking all the forms of the structure of our government without recourse to the people themselves, as provided in their own Constitution which really belongs to the people, and it does not belong to any administration.

Next, I suggest that they read their oath of office to support the Constitution of the United States, and I ask them to remember that they took that oath with their hands on the Holy Bible, thereby calling upon God Almighty himself to witness their solemn promise. It is bad enough to disappoint us.

Sixth, I suggest that from this moment on they resolve to make the Constitution again the Civil Bible of the United States and to pay it the same civil respect and reverence that they would religiously pay the Holy Scripture, and I ask them to read from the Holy Scripture the paragraph of the prodigal son, and to follow his example. "Stop, stop wasting your substance in a foreign land and come back to your father's house."

Now, in conclusion, let me give this solemn warning: There can be only one capital, Washington or Moscow.

There can be only one atmosphere of government, the clear, pure, fresh air of free America, or the foul breath of communistic Russia. There can be only one flag, the Stars and Stripes, or the flag of the godless Union of the Soviets. There can be only one national anthem, "The Star-Spangled Banner," or the "Internationale."

There can be only one victor. If the Constitution wins, we win.

But if the Constitution—stop, stop there—the Constitution can't lose.

The fact is, it has already won, but the news has not reached certain ears.[6]

HUEY LONG: FDR, BETRAYER OF THE MASSES

As FDR approached the end of his first term, he found that one of his most vitriolic critics—and potentially most dangerous rivals— was Huey Long, U.S. Senator from Louisiana, and founder of Share- the-Wealth clubs which swept across the nation after 1934. Long advocated a more equal distribution of income in the United States and charged that FDR had gone back on his campaign promises of 1932 to help the masses. Long's increasing power and popularity in 1934 and 1935 created pressures which undoubtedly led FDR to move further to the Left during these years and to support social legislation. An extraordinarily effective orator, Long's radio address excerpted below conveys some of his dynamism and wide-ranging appeal.

Ladies and gentlemen, it has been publicly announced that the White House orders of the Roosevelt administration have declared war on Huey Long. The late and lamented, the pampered ex-crown prince, Gen. Hugh S. Johnson, one of those satellites loaned by Wall Street to run the Government, and who, at the end of his control over and dismissal from the N. R. A., pronounced it "as dead as a dodo," this Mr. Johnson was apparently selected to make the lead-off speech in this White House charge begun last Monday night. The Johnson speech was followed by more fuss and fury on behalf of the administration by spell-blinders in and out of Congress.

In a far-away island, when a queen dies, her first favorite is done the honor to be buried alive with her. The funeral procession of the N. R. A. (another one of these new-deal schisms or isms) is about ready to occur. It is said that General Johnson's speech of Monday night to attack me

[6] *The New York Times,* January 26, 1936.

was delivered on the eve of announcing the publication of his obituary in the Red Book Magazine. Seems then that soon this erstwhile prince of the deranged alphabet makes ready to appear at the funeral of N. R. A. like unto the colored lady in Mississippi who there asserted: "I is de wife of dese remains."

I shall undertake to cover my main subject and make answer to these gentlemen in the course of this speech tonight.

It will serve no purpose to our distressed people for me to call my opponents more bitter names than they call me. Even were I able, I have not the time to present my side of the argument and match them in billingsgate or profanity.

What is this trouble with this administration of Mr. Roosevelt, Mr. Johnson, Mr. Farley, Mr. Astor, and all their spoilers and spellbinders? They think that Huey Long is the cause of all their worry. They go gunning for me. But, am I the cause of their misery? They are like old Davy Crockett, who went out to hunt a possum. He saw in the gleam of the moonlight that a possum in the top of a tree was going from limb to limb. He shot and missed. He saw the possum again. He fired a second time and missed again. Soon he discovered that it was not a possum he saw at all in the top of that tree. It was a louse in his own eyebrow.

I do not make this illustration to do discredit to any of these gentlemen. I make it to show how often we imagine we see great trouble being done to us by someone at a distance, when, in reality, all of it may be a fault in our own make-up.

The trouble with the Roosevelt administration is that when their schemes and isms have failed, these things I told them not to do and voted not to do, that they think it will help them to light out on those of us who warned them in the beginning that the tangled messes and noble experiments would not work. The Roosevelt administration has had its way for 2 years. They have been allowed to set up or knock down anything and everybody. There was one difference between Hoover and Roosevelt. Hoover could not get the Congress to carry out the schemes he wanted to try. We managed to lick him on a roll call in the United States Senate time after time. But, different with Mr. Roosevelt. He got his plans through Congress. But on cold analysis they were found to be the same things Hoover tried to pass and failed.

The kitchen cabinet that sat in to advise Hoover was not different from the kitchen cabinet which advised Roosevelt. Many of the persons are the same. Many of those in Roosevelt's kitchen cabinet are of the same men or set of men who furnished employees to sit in the kitchen cabinet to advise Hoover.

Maybe you see a little change in the man waiting on the tables, but back in the kitchen the same set of cooks are fixing up the victuals for us that cooked up the mess under Hoover.

Why, do you think this Roosevelt's plan for plowing up cotton, corn, and wheat; and for pouring milk in the river, and for destroying and burying hogs and cattle by the millions, all while people starve and go naked—do you think those plans were the original ideas of this Roosevelt administration? If you do, you are wrong. The whole idea of that kind of thing first came from Hoover's administration. Don't you remember when Mr. Hoover proposed to plow up every fourth row of cotton? We laughed him into scorn. President Roosevelt flayed him for proposing such a thing in the speech which he made from the steps of the capitol in Topeka, Kans.

And so we beat Mr. Hoover on his plan. But when Mr. Roosevelt started on his plan, it was not to plow up every fourth row of cotton as Hoover tried to do. Roosevelt's plan was to plow up every third row of cotton, just one-twelfth more cotton to be plowed up than Hoover proposed. Roosevelt succeeded in his plan.

So it has been that while millions have starved and gone naked; so it has been that while babies have cried and died for milk; so it has been that while people have begged for meat and bread, Mr. Roosevelt's administration has sailed merrily along, plowing under and destroying the things to eat and to wear, with tear-dimmed eyes and hungry souls made to chant for this new deal so that even their starvation dole is not taken away, and meanwhile the food and clothes craved by their bodies and souls go for destruction and ruin. What is it? Is it government? Maybe so. It looks more like St. Vitus dance.

Now, since they sallied forth with General Johnson to start the war on me, let us take a look at this N. R. A. that they opened up around here 2 years ago. They had parades and Fascist signs just as Hitler, and Mussolini. They started the dictatorship here to regiment business and labor much more than anyone did in Germany or Italy. The only difference was in the sign. Italy's sign of the Fascist was a black shirt. Germany's sign of the Fascist was a swastika. So in America they sidetracked the Stars and Stripes, and the sign of the Blue Eagle was used instead.

And they proceeded with the N. R. A. Everything from a peanut stand to a power house had to have a separate book of rules and laws to regulate what they did. If a peanut stand started to parch a sack of goobers for sale, they had to be careful to go through the rule book. One slip and he went to jail. A little fellow who pressed a pair of pants went to jail because he charged 5 cents under the price set in the rule book. So they wrote their N. R. A. rule book, codes, laws, etc. They got up over 900 of them. One would be as thick as an unabridged dictionary and as confusing as a study of the stars. It would take 40 lawyers to tell a shoe-shine stand how to operate and be certain he didn't go to jail.

Some people came to me for advice, as a lawyer, on how to run a busi-ness. I took several days and then couldn't understand it myself. The only thing I could tell them was that it couldn't be much worse in jail than it was out of jail with that kind of thing going on in the country, and so to go on and do the best they could.

The whole thing of Mr. Roosevelt, as run under General Johnson, be-came such a national scandal that Roosevelt had to let Johnson slide out as the scapegoat. Let them call for an N. R. A. parade tomorrow and you couldn't get enough people to form a funeral march.

It was under this N. R. A. and the other funny alphabetical combina-tions which followed it that we ran the whole country into a mares nest. The Farley and Johnsons combed the land with agents, inspectors, super-visors, detectives, secretaries, assistants, etc., all armed with the power to arrest and send to jail whomever they found not living up to some rule in one of these 900 catalogs. One man whose case reached the Supreme Court of the United States was turned loose because they couldn't even find the rule he was supposed to have violated in a search throughout the United States.

And now it is with P. W. A.'s, C. W. A.'s, N. R. A.'s, A. A. A.'s, J-U G's, G-I N's, and every other flimsy combination that the country finds its affairs and business tangled to where no one can recognize it. More men are now out of work than ever; the debt of the United States has gone up another $10,000,000,000. There is starvation; there is homeless-ness; there is misery on every hand and corner, but mind you, in the meantime, Mr. Roosevelt has had his way. He is one man that can't blame any of his troubles on Huey Long. He has had his way. Down in my part of the country, if any man has the measles he blames that on me; but there is one man that can't blame anything on anybody but himself, and that is Mr. Franklin De-La-No Roose-velt.

And now, on top of that, they order war on me because nearly 4 years ago I told Hoover's crowd it wouldn't do and because 3 years ago I told Roosevelt and his crowd it wouldn't do. In other words, they are in a rage at Huey Long because I have said, "I told you so."

I am not overstating the conditions now prevailing in this country. In their own words they have confessed all I now say or ever have said. Mr. Roosevelt and even Mrs. Roosevelt have bewailed the fact that food, clothes, and shelter have not been provided for the people. Even Gen.

Hugh S. Johnson said in his speech of Monday night that there are 80,-000,000 people in America who are badly hurt or wrecked by this depression. Mr. Harry Hopkins, who runs the relief work, says the dole roll has risen now to 22,375,000 persons, the highest it has ever been. And now, what is there for the Roosevelt crowd to do but to admit the facts and admit further that they are now on their third year, making matters worse instead of better all the time? No one is to blame, except them, for what is going on because they have had their way. And if they couldn't change the thing in over 2 years, now bogged down worse than ever, how could anyone expect any good of them hereafter? God save us 2 more years of the disaster we have had under that gang.

Now, my friends, when this condition of distress and suffering among so many millions of our people began to develop in the Hoover administration, we knew then what the trouble was and what we would have to do to correct it. I was the first man to say publicly—but Mr. Roosevelt followed in my tracks a few months later and said the same thing. We said that all of our trouble and woe was due to the fact that too few of our people owned too much of our wealth. We said that in our land, with too much to eat, and too much to wear, and too many houses to live in, too many automobiles to be sold, that the only trouble was that the people suffered in the land of abundance because too few controlled the money and the wealth and too many did not have money with which to buy the things they needed for life and comfort.

So I said to the people of the United States in my speeches which I delivered in the United States Senate in the early part of 1932 that the only way by which we could restore our people to reasonable life and comfort was to limit the size of the big man's fortune and guarantee some minimum to the fortune and comfort of the little man's family.

I said then, as I have said since, that it was inhuman to have food rotting, cotton and wool going to waste, houses empty, and at the same time to have millions of our people starving, naked, and homeless because they could not buy the things which other men had and for which they had no use whatever. So we convinced Mr. Franklin Delano Roosevelt that it was necessary that he announce and promise to the American people that in the event he were elected President of the United States he would pull down the size of the big man's fortune and guarantee something to every family—enough to do away with all poverty and to give employment to those who were able to work and education to the children born into the world.

Mr. Roosevelt made those promises; he made them before he was nominated in the Chicago convention. He made them again before he was elected in November, and he went so far as to remake those promises after he was inaugurated President of the United States. And I thought for a day or two after he took the oath as President, that maybe he was going through with his promises. No heart was ever so saddened; no person's ambition was ever so blighted, as was mine when I came to the realization that the President of the United States was not going to undertake what he had said he would do, and what I knew to be necessary if the people of America were ever saved from calamity and misery.[7]

FATHER CHARLES E. COUGHLIN: FDR, TOOL OF THE MONEY POWER

After 1935 FDR was frequently attacked by America's most popular radio priest, Father Charles E. Coughlin. As head of the National Union for Social Justice, Coughlin advocated large-scale inflationary money policies and criticized FDR's timidity with currency manipulation. Perhaps as many as twelve million listeners each week heard Father Coughlin's accusations. By 1936 Coughlin had united himself with the cause of Francis Townsend, leader of the movement for federal old age pensions. Both men criticized FDR for not doing enough to help those who were suffering most severely from the depression crisis. Coughlin believed that FDR's reluctance could be traced to the influence of capitalists and financiers who held him in their grasp. The speech excerpted below is an attack on FDR which Coughlin delivered before a gathering of Townsend followers.

It is my happy privilege to be here this morning on the invitation of Dr. Townsend. I feel that I will not be able to speak to you very lengthily because I have lost my voice somewhere between Virginia and Minnesota on a tour that I was making, speaking to the officers of the National Union for Social Justice, and thus I am inflicting this rasping sound upon you at your own displeasure.

It is not my privilege to come here, ladies and gentlemen, to convince you, were it necessary to convince you, and I choose not to convince you of what resolutions you should pass at this convention.

It isn't my purpose even to endeavor to persuade you upon any future policy which you and your leaders will adopt. I come before you, however, to advise you of a few policies of the National Union for Social Justice that you may compare them, to tell you of some resolutions adopted by

---

[7] U.S., *Congressional Record*, 74th Cong., 1st Sess., 1935, [Vol. 79, pp. 3436-3437.

the National Union, in order that they may be safeguards to direct you either to follow along and examine or to reject them. . . .

Is it democracy for the President of this nation to assume power over Congress, to browbeat the Congress and to insist that his "must" legislation be passed? Is that democracy?

Or is it democracy for the President of the United States to say: "Pass this legislation whether it is constitutional or not." Is that democracy?

Is it democracy, I ask those who cling to the party of Andrew Jackson, to have our country filled with plutocrats or bureaucrats and their banks filled with unpayable debts, all to save the bankers? Is that democracy? I ask the Democrats from the South to examine the history, to learn your true Andrew Jackson, and to explore those Communists who have seized the party reins of the Democrats and who are flogging their party with destructional patronage.

I ask you to purge the man who claims to be a Democrat from the Democratic party, and I mean Franklin Double-Crossing Roosevelt. . . .

The 1932 platform of the Democratic party will take its place in the annals of American literature with the Gettysburg address of the great Lincoln. The inaugural address delivered on the streets of Washington on March 4, 1933, will be lived up to in practice at some future date and then we will have rendered complete the Gettysburg address of the emancipator, Lincoln. But the heart that conceived that platform and uttered that inaugural address has lacked that divine spark known to human children of the Lord, the spark of truthfulness and the spark of sincerity.

As far as the National Union is concerned, no candidate which is endorsed for Congress can campaign, go electioneering for, or support the great betrayer and liar, Franklin D. Roosevelt, he who promised to drive the money changers from the temple and succeeded in driving the farmers from their homesteads and the citizens from their homes in the cities.

He who promised to drive the money changers from the temple has built up the greatest debt in all history. $35,000,000,000, which he permitted the bankers the right, without restriction, to spend, and for which he contracted that you and your children shall repay with seventy billion hours of labor to farms, to factories or places of business.

Seven seconds to coin the money and seventy billion hours to pay it back! Is that driving the money changers from the temple?

He who advocated the doctrine of good neighborliness with his right hand, stretched out the left to communistic Mexico where both Catholics and Protestants were assassinated for the mere act of holding up the cross. Is that good neighborliness?

For those two reasons which I have not time to amplify for you, the

National Union for Social Justice will not endorse any candidate if he is a Democrat who openly advocates the re-election of the great betrayer, Franklin Delano Roosevelt. On the other hand, ladies and gentlemen, what is our stand for the Republicans?

I am cognizant of the history following the World War. I know of their Hardings and Coolidges; of their Hoovers and their gold standards, and I know that people were prostrate—how we, following the war, canceled $14,000,000,000 of European war debts and repudiated $11,000,000,000 more of post-war debts simply to save the international bankers, simply to save the gold standard, and today Mr. Landon advocates the restoration into the nation of the gold standard. I am forced to repudiate his philosophy and his platform as a return to the days of human slavery.

It is most significant, my friends, that the hand of Moscow backs the Communist leaders in America, and aims to pledge their support for Franklin Delano Roosevelt where communism stands.

Very likely in this assemblage this morning there are some politicians who are thinking more of their jobs and their patronage than they do of Dr. Townsend and his principles. Ladies and gentlemen, you have them here.

They raise their voices at the mention of democracy, but do they know the history of democracy in America? Study Andrew Jackson and his radical personal tax. Learn about the great fellow and his work. Who brought his ideas back and on what plank? Did Jackson succeed? Why, most certainly he did, because Jackson was a man of his word.

Jackson restored to Congress the right to coin and regulate the value of money, which Alexander Hamilton stole from Congress. Shortly after Jackson died those who still believed in his philosophy in their minds, but in whose hearts there wasn't the blood to carry their beliefs through, the Old World democracy, identified themselves with the thoughts of the international bankers until they sold you out as a mess of pottage.

Is that democracy? Or what is democracy today? Is it some fact of the mind that begins at the Mason and Dixon Line and ends at the Gulf, or is it a label for political patronage with the seal, sign and stamp of "Farleyism" smeared all over it? [8]

EARL BROWDER: FDR, EXPLOITER OF THE WORKING CLASS

Some of the most savage criticism of FDR and his New Deal came from the extreme Left. Earl Browder, a prominent leader of the American Communist Party during the 1930's, castigated the New Deal as a brand of Fascism, and FDR as an authoritarian

[8] *The New York Times,* July 17, 1936.

leader, who, as spokesman for capitalists in the United States, oppressed the workers. The excerpt from Browder's book below provides an indication of the tone as well as the specific accusations which Communists in the United States were accustomed to make against FDR.

Manifesto of the Communist Party of the United States

To All Workers of the U.S.A.:

We speak to you in the name of 25,000 members of the Communist Party who elected the delegates of this Eighth National Convention; in the name of several hundred thousand workers who elected fraternal delegates from trade unions, unemployment councils, workers' clubs, fraternal societies; in the name of the miners, steel workers, metal workers, auto workers, textile workers, marine workers, railroad workers, whose delegates constitute a majority of this convention.

To you, the working class and toiling farmers of the United States, this Convention of workers addresses itself, to speak a few plain words about the crisis, and about the possibility of finding a way out.

The crisis of the capitalist system is becoming more and more a catastrophe for the workers and toiling masses. Growing millions of the exploited population are faced with increased difficulties in finding the barest means of livelihood. Unemployment relief is being drastically cut and in many cases abolished altogether. Real wages are being reduced further every month, and labor is being speeded up to an inhuman degree.

The vast majority of the poor farmers are slowly but surely being squeezed off the land and thrown on the "free" labor market to compete with the workers. The oppressed Negro people are loaded down with the heaviest economic burdens, especially of unemployment, denied even the crumbs of relief given to the starving white masses, and further subjected to bestial lynch law and Jim-Crowism. Women workers and housewives are especially sufferers from the crisis, and from the fascist movements to drive them out of industry. Millions of young workers are thrown upon the streets by the closing of schools and simultaneously are denied any chance to earn their living in the industries.

The suffering masses have been told to look to Washington for their salvation. Mr. Roosevelt and his New Deal have been decked out with the rainbow promises of returning prosperity. But the bitter truth is rapidly being learned that Roosevelt and his New Deal represent the Wall Street bankers and big corporations—finance capital—just the same as Hoover before him, but carrying out even fiercer attacks against the living standards of the masses of the people. Under Roosevelt and the

New Deal policies, the public treasury has been turned into a huge trough where the big capitalists eat their fill. Over ten billion dollars have been handed out to the banks and corporations, billions have been squeezed out of the workers and farmers by inflation and by all sorts of new taxes upon the masses. Under the Roosevelt regime, the main burden of taxation has been shifted away from the big capitalists onto the impoverished masses.

The N.R.A. and the industrial codes have served further to enrich the capitalists by establishing fixed monopoly prices, speeding up trustification, and squeezing out the smaller capitalists and independent producers.

The labor provisions of the N.R.A., which were hailed by the A. F. of L. and Socialist leaders as "a new charter for labor," have turned out in reality to be new chains for labor. The fixing of the so-called minimum wage, at below starvation levels, has turned out in reality to be a big effort to drive the maximum wage down to this point. The so-called guarantee of the right to organize and collective bargaining has turned out in reality to be the establishment of company unions. The last remaining rights of the workers they now propose to take away by establishing compulsory arbitration under the Wagner Bill, camouflaged as an attempt to guarantee workers' rights. Roosevelt has given official governmental status to the company unions, in the infamous "settlement" in the auto industry. This new step toward fascism is announced as a "new course" to apply to all industries.

All these domestic policies are openly recognized as identical in their content with the measures of professed fascist governments. This rapid movement toward fascism in the United States goes hand in hand with the sharpening of international antagonisms and the most gigantic preparations for war ever before witnessed in a pre-war period. More than a billion dollars have been appropriated for war purposes during this year. A large proportion of this has been taken directly out of the funds ostensibly appropriated for public works. Hundreds of millions are being spent on military training in the so-called Civil Conservation Camps, run by the War Department.

The policies of the government in Washington have one purpose, to make the workers and farmers and middle classes pay the costs of the crisis, to preserve the profits of the big capitalists at all costs, to establish fascism at home and to wage imperialist war abroad.[9]

This world situation is the outgrowth of the deepening of the crisis of world capitalism. This is bringing profound changes into the world relationships and into the domestic policies of the American bourgeoisie.

[9] Earl Browder, *Communism in the United States* (New York, 1935), pp. 13-14.

In the United States these changes are expressed in the development of the Roosevelt "New Deal."

The "New Deal" represents the rapid development of bourgeois policy under the blows of the crisis, the sharpening of the class struggle at home and the imminence of a new imperialist war. The "New Deal" is a policy of slashing the living standards at home and fighting for markets abroad, for the simple purpose of maintaining the profits of finance capital. It is a policy of brutal oppression at home and of imperialist war abroad. It represents a further sharpening and deepening of the world crisis.

It has become very fashionable lately to speak about the "New Deal" as American fascism. One of Mussolini's newspapers declares that Roosevelt is following the path marked out by Italian fascism.

Norman Thomas has contributed a profound thought to the question and has written several long articles in the capitalist press, to point out that the "New Deal" is "economic fascism," and that it is composed of good and bad elements, many of them even "progressive" in their nature, if not accompanied by "political reaction." And a group of honest revolutionary workers in Brooklyn recently issued a leaflet in which they declared that Roosevelt and Hitler are the same thing. Such answers as these to the question of the essential character of the "New Deal" will not help us much.

It is true that elements of fascism long existing in America are being greatly stimulated, and are coming to maturity more rapidly than ever before. But it would be well for us to recall the analysis of fascism made at the Eleventh and Twelfth Plenums of the Executive Committee of the Communist International, both for the purpose of understanding the situation in Germany and for accurately judging the developments in America.

First, it must be understood that fascism grows naturally out of bourgeois democracy under the conditions of capitalist decline. It is only another form of the same class rule, the dictatorship of finance capital. Only in this sense can one say that Roosevelt is the same as Hitler, in that both are executives of finance capital. The same thing, however, could be said of every other executive of every other capitalist state. To label everything capitalist as fascism results in destroying all distinction between the various forms of capitalist rule. If we should raise these distinctions to a level of difference in principle, between fascism on the one side and bourgeois democracy on the other, this would be following in the line of reformism, of social-fascism. But on the other hand to ignore entirely these distinctions would be tactical stupidity, would be an example of "left" doctrinairism.

Second: the growth of fascist tendencies is a sign of the weakening of the rule of finance capital. It is a sign of the deepening of the crisis, a sign that finance capital can no longer rule in the old forms. It must turn to the more open and brutal and terroristic methods, not as the exception but as the rule, for the oppression of the population at home and preparation for war abroad. It is preventive counter-revolution, an attempt to head off the rise of the revolutionary upsurge of the masses.

Third: fascism is not a special economic system. Its economic measures go no further in the modification of the capitalist economic forms than all capitalist classes have always gone under the exceptional stresses of war and preparation for war. The reason for the existence of fascism is to protect the economic system of capitalism, private property in the means of production, the basis of the rule of finance capital.

Fourth: fascism comes to maturity with the direct help of the Socialist Parties, the parties of the Second International, who are those elements within the working class we describe as social-fascists because of the historic role which they play. Under the mask of opposition to fascism, they in reality pave the way for fascism to come to power. They disarm the workers by the theory of the lesser evil; they tell the workers they will be unable to seize and hold power; they create distrust in the revolutionary road by means of slanders against the Soviet Union; they throw illusions of democracy around the rising forces of fascism; they break up the international solidarity of the workers. They carry this out under the mask of "socialism" and "Marxism." In America this role is played by the S.P., "left" reformists and the A. F. of L. bureaucracy.

The development of Roosevelt's program is a striking illustration of the fact that there is no Chinese wall between democracy and fascism. Roosevelt operates with all of the arts of "democratic" rule, with an emphasized liberal and social-demagogic cover, quite a contrast with Hoover who was outspokenly reactionary. Yet behind this smoke screen, Roosevelt is carrying out more thoroughly, more brutally than Hoover, the capitalist attack against the living standards of the masses and the sharpest national chauvinism in foreign relations.[10]

ADOLPH HITLER: FDR, WARMONGER

Few men hated FDR more intensely than Adolph Hitler, the Fuehrer of fascist Germany. In assessing the blame for the outbreak of World War II, and for American participation, Hitler pointed his vengeful finger directly at the President. In his speech to the German Parliament a few days after the United States declared war

[10] Earl Browder, *Communism in the United States* (New York, 1935), pp. 114-117.

*on Germany, Hitler gave vent to his emotions and charged FDR
with responsibility for the world conflict.*

The first question that we face is why this man (FDR) has such a
fanatical hatred for our country when in its entire history it has never
harmed either himself or his own nation.

*   *   *

America is a republic led by a powerful chief executive. Germany was
once a limited monarchy, later a democracy without power, today a strong
republic. An ocean lies between the two countries. The differences between capitalist America and bolshevik Russia are far greater—if the
simile is at all valid—than those between an American led by a strong
president and a Germany led by a Fuehrer.

But it is a fact that the two wars between Germany and the United
States—even if inspired by the same force [Jews]—were begun by two
Americans, Presidents Wilson and Franklin Roosevelt.

Judgment on Wilson has been passed by history. His name remains
synonymous with the worst epithets of all time. The consequence of his
lies was the shattering of the lives not only of the vanquished nations, but
of the victors themselves. . . .

What is the reason, after such bitter experiences, which leads a president of the United States to see his sole task as allowing wars to break
out, and above all, to agitate hostility against Germany? National Socialism achieved power in Germany during the same year that Roosevelt was
elected president of the United States. It is important to analyze the reasons for the present situation.

First, the personal equation. I am well aware of the fact that there is
a world of difference in my approach to things and that of President
Roosevelt. Roosevelt hails from an enormously wealthy family, and belongs to the class whose path is eased by their birth and social position in
a democracy. I myself was only a child in a small and poor family and
had to fight for everything with unbounded energy and diligence. When
the World War came, Roosevelt lived through it as a non-combatant
through the good offices of Wilson. Thus he knows only the positive aspects of war, characteristic of those who profit in business while others
bleed to death.

During this same period my life was very different. I did not belong
with those who made history or engaged in business, but I carried out
orders. As a common soldier I made an effort during these four years to

carry out my responsibilities against the enemy, and thus I returned from the war just as poor as I entered it in the autumn of 1914. I shared my fate with millions of others while Mr. Roosevelt shared it with the so-called upper ten thousand. While after the war Mr. Roosevelt tried his abilities as a financial speculator in order to gain personal profit from inflationary trends, I, like many hundred thousands of others, was still lying in the hospital. And when at last Mr. Roosevelt began his career as a politician—backed by Big Business—I fought, as an anonymous unknown, for the rebirth of my nation which was subjected to the greatest injustice of its entire history.

Two ways of life! When Franklin Roosevelt assumed the leadership of the United States he was the candidate of a capitalistic political party which he served. And when I became Prime Minister of Germany I became the leader of a national movement which I myself created.

The powers which sustained Mr. Roosevelt were the powers which I fight—out of my most sacred inner convictions, on grounds relating to the destiny of my people. The "Brain Trust" which the new American President had to use consisted of members of that same race [Jews] which we fight because they are a parasitic manifestation of the human race who need to be removed from public life.

And yet both of us had something in common. Franklin Roosevelt took over a nation which had collapsed economically because of democratic government, and I took over leadership of the Reich which—due to the influence of democracy—also found itself on the brink of ruin. The United States had 13 million unemployed, Germany had 7 million in addition to seven million part-time workers. In both countries public finances had collapsed, and the total disruption of economic life seemed hardly unavoidable.

At this moment there occurred the development of trends in the United States and in Germany about which future generations will cast the final judgment. While under National Socialist leadership Germany experienced an enormous recovery in just a few years, in economy, culture, art, etc., President Roosevelt was unable even to secure a slight improvement of conditions in his own country.

*   *   *

A threatening opposition to the Roosevelt policies began to form. It intimated that he could be saved only by drawing public opinion from attention on domestic policy to foreign affairs. It is interesting to study the despatches of the Polish ambassador to Washington, Potocki, which draw attention to the fact that Roosevelt was conscious of the collapse of his entire economic house of cards and that he saw it necessary there-fore to divert attention to foreign policy.

* * *

Especially vindictive was his policy against Germany. After 1937 he began a systematic campaign in his speeches to arouse hatred of public opinion against Germany, particularly his nasty address of October 5, 1937. He threatened the establishment of some kind of quarantine against the so-called authoritarian states. In carrying out this increasing policy of hate and agitation he recalled the American ambassador to Berlin. Since then both states were represented only by special envoys. After November, 1938, he began consciously to sabotage peace-making efforts in Europe. In so doing he two-facedly pretended to be interested in peace, but threatens any nation which is peacefully inclined with economic sanctions, freezing of funds, cancellation of loans, and so on. In this in-stance we glimpse the realities through the despatches of the Polish am-bassadors in Washington, London, Paris, and Brussels. In January, 1939 this man intensifies his campaign of agitation and before Congress threat-ens the authoritarian states with all means short of war. While he insists continually that other countries seek to interfere in American affairs, and while he seeks to uphold the Monroe Doctrine, in March of 1939 he be-gins to mix in European affairs which are no business of the President of the United States. In the first place, he does not understand any of these problems; secondly, even if he understood them he would have just as little right to concern himself with Central Europe as the German chief of state would have regarding one of the states within the United States.

Yes, Mr. Roosevelt goes even further. Against all principles of interna-tional law he declares that he will not recognize any governments which he does not like, nor new arrangements; that he will continue to recog-nize diplomats from states which no longer exist and even to recognize their governments as legal. On April 15, 1939, Roosevelt sent his famous message to me and the Duce which revealed a mixture of geographic and political ignorance related to the arrogance of one who belonged to the class of millionaires. It ordered us to make declarations and non-aggres-sion treaties with innumerable states, many of which no longer had their independence because they were annexed by the allies of Mr. Roosevelt, or were made protectorates by them.

At that point his genial wife joined him in his stance. She declined to live with her son in a world which we own. That is at least understand-able. Because this is a world in which work counts, not cheating or ma-nipulation. But after a short rest, on November 4, 1939, this man secures for his wife an amendment of the neutrality laws to lift the prohibition on arms exports largely to favor the enemies of Germany. . . .

After July, 1940, Roosevelt intensifies the measures which carry the United States to war by allowing Americans to join the British air force and by educating English pilots in the United States. And already in 1940 he undertook establishment of a joint military program between the United States and Canada. In order to make the creation of an American-Canadian defense committee plausible, from time to time he invents crises in which he acts as if America were threatened by an attack. . . .

The insulting attacks which this so-called president has directed against me personally I will forego mentioning; it makes no difference to me if he calls me a gangster, especially since this term originated in the United States and not in Europe. But, apart from that, Mr. Roosevelt cannot in any way insult me since I consider him to be mentally ill like Woodrow Wilson. It is clear to us that this man and his Jewish associates have been agitating against Japan in very similar fashion. . . .

First he provokes war; then he falsifies its causes, makes extravagant claims and clothes himself in a cloud of Christian deceit. Then he leads humanity slowly but surely to war, but not without calling upon God as a judge of his actions. . . .[11]

HENRY L. STIMSON: FDR, WAR LEADER

During World War II few Cabinet members were closer to FDR than Henry L. Stimson, his Secretary of War. When Stimson observed FDR in his role as Commander-in-Chief, he was not always happy over FDR's administrative methods, but he did admire his grasp of military and political goals.

The history of war production showed the President's administrative technique at every stage. Having tinkered for nearly two years with boards and commissions, he finally gave real power to the wrong man. Then when that man got into trouble, the President coasted along; he neither fully backed Mr. Nelson nor fired him. Stimson believed that it was Mr. Roosevelt's irritated but indecisive tolerance of men lacking strength of character that lay behind many wartime administrative difficulties. Dis-

[11] Adolph Hitler, [*Speech of the Fuehrer Concerning the War Guilt of Franklin D. Roosevelt*] Delivered to the Reichstag, December 11, 1941 (Berlin, 1942). Trans. G. D. Nash.

agreements with men like Hull and Morgenthau were painful, but in these cases Stimson always knew where he stood; disagreements with men who backed and filled were extremely irritating.

In March 1943, after several months of friction in the government, Stimson took time out to register a summary complaint to his diary. After acquitting Mr. Roosevelt of the charge of playing politics with the war effort, he continued:

"But the President is the poorest administrator I have ever worked under in respect to the orderly procedure and routine of his performance. He is not a good chooser of men and he does not know how to use them in co-ordination.

"When I last held the post of Secretary of War under Mr. Taft, who was a very good administrator, there were only nine cabinet officers, or ten persons at the cabinet table including the President. Barring the Interstate Commerce Commission and perhaps one or two other minor quasi-independent commissions, every administrative function headed up in one of the nine cabinet officers and went to the President through the departmental head. Mr. Taft dealt with his departments through his Cabinet and that gave you a sense of responsibility and security that could not otherwise be obtained. Today the President has constituted an almost innumerable number of new administrative posts, putting at the head of them a lot of inexperienced men appointed largely for personal grounds and who report on their duties directly to the President and have constant and easy access to him. The result is that there are a lot of young men in Washington ambitious to increase the work of their agencies and having better access to the President than his cabinet officers have. The lines of delimitation between these different agencies themselves and between them and the Departments [are] very nebulous. The inevitable result is that the Washington atmosphere is full of acrimonious disputes over matters of jurisdiction. In my own case, a very large percentage of my time and strength, particularly of recent months, has been taken up in trying to smooth out and settle the differences which have been thus created." (Diary, March 28, 1943.)

Whatever his weaknesses as an administrator, however, the President had a firm understanding of the facts of war. His underlings might wish to give antitrust suits precedence over war production, but the President was not persuaded. Publicity-seeking officials might wish to turn a military trial of saboteurs into a public spectacle, in spite of the fact that these same officials had informed the War Department that much of the evidence would be valuable to the enemy; the President stood firm. In some of these matters, and notably in his impatience with irresponsible sections of the press, Mr. Roosevelt was indeed more vigorous than his Secretary of War. . . .[12]

After the war, considering such problems as those just discussed, Stimson was reinforced in his wartime belief that Mr. Roosevelt's personal virtuosity in high politics carried with it certain disadvantages which might have been limited if the President had been willing to provide himself with a War Cabinet for the co-ordinated execution of his policies —a body which might have done in war diplomacy what the Joint Chiefs of Staff did in military strategy.

Problems like those of China and France were not merely diplomatic— the State Department could not and would not assume the whole labor of determining policy in areas where the military interest was so significant. Yet the military interest could not of itself be wholly determinant; it was not proper that such questions should be decided by the Joint Chiefs of Staff, as the members of that body well understood.

Mr. Roosevelt therefore could not rely on his regularly constituted advisers—military or diplomatic—for final recommendation and coordinated execution in problems of war diplomacy. Nor were his regular cabinet meetings a suitable place for such discussion and decision; there were nearly twenty men in cabinet meetings, and during the war they became a formality; to Stimson they were useful principally as a way of getting into the White House to have a word with the President in private after the meetings were over; a typical diary entry describes a cabinet meeting toward the end of the war as "the same old two-and-sixpence, no earthly good." Mr. Roosevelt's own view of cabinet meetings was not wholly different: "The cabinet meeting this afternoon was brief. The President opened it by saying humorously that he had just told his family that he wanted a short cabinet meeting and they had said, 'Well, you know how you can get it. You can just stop your own talking.' There was a smile around the table because of the truth of the statement. The Roosevelt Cabinets are really a solo performance by the President interspersed with some questions and very few debates. . . ." (Diary, May 1, 1942). . . .[13]

The proper solution, Stimson believed, would have been for Mr. Roosevelt to provide himself with a War Cabinet like that upon which Winston Churchill relied in Great Britain. Cabinet responsibility, of course, is not the same in the United States as in Great Britain, but Stimson felt that

[12] Henry L. Stimson and McGeorge Bundy, *On Active Service in Peace and War* (New York, 1948), pp. 494-496.
[13] *Ibid.*, pp. 561-562.

Mr. Roosevelt would have found it helpful to have some such body for the handling of his war policies in foreign lands. Such a body would have included his most trusted personal adviser, Harry Hopkins, and perhaps the Secretaries of State, Treasury, War, and Navy. Organized like the Joint Chiefs of Staff, with a secretariat of top quality and a continuing record of the policy decisions made or approved by the President, such a body might have avoided some, at least, of the difficulties discussed above, and others not unlike them in other areas. Stimson would never have desired that the President's personal initiative and extraordinary talent should be limited by red tape, but he felt sure that such a body would have been a reinforcement to Mr. Roosevelt's less evident abilities as a co-ordinator and executive. Unfortunately the whole idea was foreign to the President's nature; only reluctantly had he accepted the notion of such an organization even in the purely military field, and he never showed the least disposition to alter his methods in diplomacy. Stimson himself never recommended a War Cabinet to Mr. Roosevelt; he had no desire to appear to push himself forward. But others made such a recommendation, and the President was not impressed.

To be useful, such a body would have had to be the President's own creation. No attempt to co-ordinate action on any lower level could have much value so long as the central threads of policy were personally managed in the White House. Back in 1940, in an effort to fill a gap which he felt at once on his arrival in Washington—and which he had noticed from the other side of the fence when he was Secretary of State—Stimson had been the leading spirit in setting up regular weekly meetings of Hull, Knox, and himself. These meetings were wholly unofficial and personal. They served a useful purpose in keeping the three Secretaries informed of one another's major problems. But they had no connection with Mr. Roosevelt's final determinations of policy, and in 1942 and 1943 they became less and less valuable. Reorganized late in 1944, with McCloy as recorder and with formal agenda and conclusions, this Committee of Three became more useful; Stimson, Stettinius, and Forrestal were able to use it for the solution of some important points and they were able to establish at a lower level, for routine co-ordination, the extremely useful State, War, and Navy Co-ordinating Committee. But the Committee of Three, in considering major problems, always remained more of a clearinghouse than an executive committee.

Another embryonic War Cabinet had existed before Pearl Harbor— the War Council, which met at frequent intervals in the White House. This group included Hull, Stimson, and Knox in addition to the senior military officers. But when Mr. Roosevelt learned to like the Joint Chiefs of Staff, in 1942, he allowed himself to dispense with any general meetings on war policy.

Stimson's belief in this notion of a War Cabinet was based partly on hindsight, and he knew that he might seem to be elevating his personal feelings into a theory of government. He hoped this was not the case. He had served in too many cabinets to expect that all decisions would match his advice, and it was not his disagreements with the President on details of policy that bothered him, as he looked back in 1947; it was rather that Mr. Roosevelt's policy was so often either unknown or not clear to those who had to execute it, and worse yet, in some cases it seemed self-contradictory. In the case of China, for example, all those who worked so energetically at cross-purposes in Chungking undoubtedly regarded themselves as possessors of a mandate from Washington—and even from the White House.

In summary, then, Stimson's experience of the diplomacy of coalition warfare in World War II left him with this conclusion: Franklin Roosevelt as a wartime international leader proved himself as good as one man could be—but one man was not enough to keep track of so vast an undertaking. . . .[14]

On the whole, Stimson was content to stand, in his judgment of President Roosevelt, on a letter written just after his death:

April 16, 1945

My dear Mrs. Roosevelt:

The sudden breaking off of the official ties which I have enjoyed with your husband and with you is a very great shock and grief to me. In the midst of it I find it very difficult to adequately express the affection and honor which I have held for you both. I have never received from any chief, under whom I served, more consideration and kindness than I did from him, even when he was laboring under the terrific strain of a great war and in spite of the fact that I was a newcomer in his Cabinet and a member of another party. He thus made natural and easy relations which might otherwise have been difficult. Out of these his characteristics grew the very real and deep affection which I came to have for him.

He was an ideal war commander in chief. His vision of the broad problems of the strategy of the war was sound and accurate, and his relations to his military advisers and commanders were admirably correct. In the execution of their duties he gave them freedom, backed them up, and held them responsible. In all these particulars he seems to me to have been our greatest war President. And his courage and cheeriness in times

[14] *Ibid.,* pp. 562-564.

of great emergency won for him the loyalty and affection of all who served under him.

Lastly and most important, his vision and interpretations of the mission of our country to help establish a rule of freedom and justice in this world raised a standard which put the United States in the unique position of world leadership which she now holds. Such facts must constitute priceless memories to you now in your sad bereavement. You may well hold your head high to have been his worthy helpmate at such a time and in such a task.

With very deep respect and affection, I am

Very sincerely yours,

HENRY L. STIMSON [15]

JOSEPH STALIN: FDR, PLUNDERER

Although the Allies and their leaders maintained an outward harmony throughout World War II, many stresses and strains beset the Grand Alliance. The Russians especially tended to distrust Great Britain and the United States. In his less guarded moments, Premier Stalin of the Soviet Union unabashedly expressed his apprehensions. After the war, in conversations with the well-known Yugoslav Communist, Milovan Djilas, Stalin charged Churchill and FDR with trickery and deceit, and with being outright thieves. Excerpts from Stalin's remarks to Djilas appear below.

Apparently encouraged by my optimism regarding the final outcome of the current German offensive against Tito, [Stalin] then took up our relations with the Allies, primarily with Great Britain, which constituted, as it appeared to me even then, the principal reason for the meeting with me.

The substance of his suggestions was, on the one hand, that we ought not to "frighten" the English, by which he meant that we ought to avoid anything that might alarm them into thinking that a revolution was going on in Yugoslavia or an attempt at Communist control. "What do you want with red stars on your caps? The form is not important but what is gained, and you—red stars! By God, stars aren't necessary!" Stalin exclaimed angrily.

But he did not hide the fact that his anger was not very great. It was a reproach, and I explained to him: "It is impossible to discontinue the red stars because they are already a tradition and have acquired a certain meaning among our fighters."

Standing by his opinion, but without great insistence, he turned to relations with the Western Allies from another aspect, and continued, "Perhaps you think that just because we are allies of the English that we have forgotten who they are and who Churchill is. They find nothing sweeter than to trick their allies. During the First World War they constantly tricked the Russians and the French. And Churchill? Churchill is the kind who, if you don't watch him, will slip a kopeck out of your pocket. Yes, a kopeck out of your pocket! By God, a kopeck out of your pocket! And Roosevelt? Roosevelt is not like that. He dips in his hand only for bigger coins. But Churchill? Churchill—even for a kopeck." [16]

WINSTON S. CHURCHILL: FDR, LEADER OF THE FREE WORLD

FDR's death was mourned by millions throughout the world who felt almost as if they had lost a friend. Few were able to express their feelings as fully, however, as Winston Churchill, one of the masters of the English language. When he reviewed the details of FDR's career he summed up what he considered to be the high spots of his life. To Churchill it seemed that FDR embodied many outstanding qualities of leadership which were put to outstanding use during World War II, providing guidance for the Allied nations.

"My friendship with the great man to whose work and fame we pay our tribute today began and ripened during this war. I had met him, but only for a few minutes, after the close of the last war, and as soon as I went to the Admiralty in September 1939 he telegraphed inviting me to correspond with him direct on naval or other matters if at any time I felt inclined. Having obtained the permission of the Prime Minister, I did so. Knowing President Roosevelt's keen interest in sea warfare, I furnished him with a stream of information about our naval affairs, and about the various actions, including especially the action of the Plate River, which lighted the first gloomy winter of the war.

"When I became Prime Minister, and the war broke out in all its hideous fury, when our own life and survival hung in the balance, I was already in a position to telegraph to the President on terms of an association which had become most intimate, and to me most agreeable. This continued through all the ups and downs of the world struggle until Thursday last, when I received my last messages from him. These messages showed no falling-off in his accustomed clear vision and vigour upon perplexing and complicated matters. I may mention that this correspondence, which of course was greatly increased after the United States' entry into the war, comprises, to and fro between us, over seventeen hundred messages. Many of these were lengthy messages, and the majority dealt with those more difficult points which come to be discussed upon the level of heads of Governments only after official solutions have not been reached at other stages. To this correspondence there must be added our nine meetings—at Argentia, three in Washington, at Casablanca, at Teheran, two at Quebec, and, last of all, at Yalta—comprising in all about one hundred and twenty days of close personal contact, during a great part of which I stayed with him at the White House or at his home at Hyde Park or in his retreat in the Blue Mountains, which he called Shangri-La.

"I conceived an admiration for him as a statesman, a man of affairs, and a war leader, I felt the utmost confidence in his upright, inspiring character and outlook, and a personal regard—affection, I must say—for him beyond my power to express today. His love of his own country, his respect for its constitution, his power of gauging the tides and currents of its mobile public opinion, were always evident, but added to these were the beatings of that generous heart which was always stirred to anger and to action by spectacles of aggression and oppression by the strong against the weak. It is indeed a loss, a bitter loss to humanity, that those heartbeats are stilled for ever.

"President Roosevelt's physical affliction lay heavily upon him. It was a marvel that he bore up against it through all the many years of tumult and storm. Not one man in ten millions, stricken and crippled as he was, would have attempted to plunge into a life of physical and mental exertion and of hard, ceaseless political controversy. Not one in ten millions would have tried, not one in a generation would have succeeded, not only in entering this sphere, not only in acting vehemently in it, but in becoming indisputable master of the scene. In this extraordinary effort of the spirit over the flesh, of will-power over physical infirmity, he was inspired and sustained by that noble woman his devoted wife, whose high ideals marched with his own, and to whom the deep and respectful sympathy of the House of Commons flows out today in all fullness. "There is no doubt that the President foresaw the great dangers closing in upon the pre-war world with far more prescience than most well-informed people on either side of the Atlantic, and that he urged forward with all his power such precautionary military preparations as peace-time opinion in the United States could be brought to accept. There never was a moment's doubt, as the quarrel opened, upon which side his sympathies lay.

The fall of France, and what seemed to most people outside this Island the impending destruction of Great Britain, were to him an agony, although he never lost faith in us. They were an agony to him not only on account of Europe, but because of the serious perils to which the United States herself would have been exposed had we been overwhelmed or the survivors cast down under the German yoke. The bearing of the British nation at that time of stress, when we were all alone, filled him and vast numbers of his countrymen with the warmest sentiments towards our people. He and they felt the Blitz of the stern winter of 1940-41, when Hitler set himself to 'rub out' the cities of our country, as much as any of us did, and perhaps more indeed, for imagination is often more torturing than reality. There is no doubt that the bearing of the British, and above all the Londoners, kindled fires in American bosoms far harder to quench than the conflagrations from which we were suffering. There was also at that time, in spite of General Wavell's victories—all the more indeed because of the reinforcements which were sent from this country to him—the apprehension widespread in the United States that we should be invaded by Germany after the fullest preparation in the spring of 1941. It was in February that the President sent to England the late Mr. Wendell Willkie, who, although a political rival and an opposing candidate, felt as he did on many important points. Mr. Willkie brought a letter from Mr. Roosevelt, which the President had written in his own hand, and this letter contained the famous lines of Longfellow:

" 'Sail on, O ship of State!
Sail on, O Union, strong and great!
Humanity with all its fears,
With all the hopes of future years,
Is hanging breathless on thy fate.' "

"At about that same time he devised the extraordinary measure of assistance called Lend-Lease, which will stand forth as the most unselfish and unsordid financial act of any country in all history. The effect of this was greatly to increase British fighting power, and for all the purposes of the war effort to make us, as it were, a much more numerous community. In that autumn I met the President for the first time during the war at Argentia, in Newfoundland, and together we drew up the declaration which has since been called the Atlantic Charter, and which will, I trust, long remain a guide for both our peoples and for other peoples of the world.

"All this time, in deep and dark and deadly secrecy, the Japanese were preparing their act of treachery and greed. When next we met in Washington, Japan, Germany, and Italy had declared war upon the United States, and both our countries were in arms, shoulder to shoulder. Since then we have advanced over the land and over the sea through many difficulties and disappointments, but always with a broadening measure of success. I need not dwell upon the series of great operations which have taken place in the Western Hemisphere, to say nothing of that other immense war proceeding on the other side of the world. Nor need I speak of the plans which we made with our great Ally, Russia, at Teheran, for these have now been carried out for all the world to see.

"But at Yalta I noticed that the President was ailing. His captivating smile, his gay and charming manner, had not deserted him, but his face had a transparency, an air of purification, and often there was a far-away look in his eyes. When I took my leave of him in Alexandria harbour I must confess that I had an indefinable sense of fear that his health and his strength were on the ebb. But nothing altered his inflexible sense of duty. To the end he faced his innumerable tasks unflinching. . . . When death came suddenly upon him he had finished his mail. That portion of his day's work was done. As the saying goes, he died in harness, and we may well say in battle harness, like his soldiers, sailors, and airmen, who side by side with ours are carrying on their task to the end all over the world. What an enviable death was his! He had brought his country through the worst of its perils and the heaviest of its toils. Victory had cast its sure and steady beam upon him. . . .

"He had broadened and stabilised in the days of peace the foundations of American life and union. In war he had raised the strength, might, and glory of the great Republic to a height never attained by any nation in history. With her left hand she was leading the advance of the conquering Allied Armies into the heart of Germany, and with her right, on the other side of the globe, she was irresistibly and swiftly breaking up the power of Japan. And all the time ships, munitions, supplies, and food of every kind were aiding on a gigantic scale her Allies, great and small . . . in the course of the long struggle.

"But all this was no more than worldly power and grandeur, had it not been that the causes of human freedom and social justice, to which so much of his life had been given, added a lustre . . . which will long be discernible among men. He has left behind him a band of resolute and able men handling the numerous interrelated parts of the vast American war machine. He has left a successor who comes forward with firm step and sure conviction to carry on the task to its appointed end. For us it remains only to say that in Franklin Roosevelt there died the greatest American friend we have ever known, and the greatest champion of freedom who has ever brought help and comfort from the New World to the Old." [17]

[17] Winston Churchill, in Great Britain, *Parliamentary Debates* (Hansard), House of Commons, Fifth Series (London, 1945), Vol. 410, pp. 73-77 (April 17, 1945).

FDR APPRAISED

How have later biographers and historians viewed FDR? Generally they have tended to be less emotional, and more realistic than contemporary observers. Writers represented in Part Three have sought not so much to praise or condemn FDR as to provide a critical basis for an understanding of his personality. Their appraisals tend to be more measured, more critical, and more balanced than the recollections of most of those who knew the President. Thus, the work of the biographers and historians should contribute to the formulation of criteria with which each reader himself can judge the life and work of FDR.

5

Champion of the New Deal

In the years since his death in 1945, FDR's objectives in formulating and executing many aspects of New Deal policies have increasingly come under the scrutiny of historians. With the advantages of hindsight, historians are often able to place his actions within a much broader context than either the President himself or his contemporaries could provide. But this should not imply that greater perspective has led the students of FDR's career to unanimity in assessing his role, for they still diverge in their appraisal of his domestic programs. Despite disagreements, however, such efforts by scholars are constructive since they frequently reveal hitherto obscure aspects of FDR's personality and life.

The selections in this chapter are designed to indicate a few of the divergent historical approaches to FDR as the champion of the New Deal. Professor Richard Hofstadter considers FDR to have been moved by opportunism; Professor James M. Burns regards him as a "power broker"; Professor Arthur M. Schlesinger, Jr. considers him a masterful blend of idealist and politician. Interestingly enough, these later appraisals are not wholly dissimilar from some of the judgments made by those who knew FDR, and whose com-

ments were noted in Part Two. But by treating diverse aspects of FDR's life, they help us to unravel the complexity of his personality.

RICHARD HOFSTADTER: AN OPPORTUNIST

A rather critical appraisal of FDR's motives came from the pen of Richard Hofstadter, who viewed FDR's great flexibility and adaptability as a weakness, rather than as a virtue.

To be sick and helpless is a humiliating experience. Prolonged illness also carries the hazard of narcissistic self-absorption. It would have been easy for Roosevelt to give up his political aspirations and retire to the comfortable privacy of Hyde Park. That he refused to relinquish his normal life was testimony to his courage and determination, and also to the strength of his ambition. From his bed he resumed as many of his affairs as possible. By the spring of 1922 he was walking on crutches, sometimes venturing to his office, and after 1924, when he found the pool at Warm Springs, he made good progress in recovering his strength. Above his enfeebled legs he developed a powerful torso.

In the long run this siege of infantile paralysis added much to Roosevelt's political appeal. As a member of the overprivileged classes with a classic Groton-Harvard career he had been too much the child of fortune. Now a heroic struggle against the cruelest kind of adversity made a more poignant success story than the usual rags-to-riches theme; it was also far better adapted to democratic leadership in a period when people were tired of self-made men and their management of affairs.

There has been much speculation about the effect of Roosevelt's illness upon his sympathies. Frances Perkins, who writes of him with intelligence and detachment and who knew him before his illness as a pleasant but somewhat supercilious young man, feels that he underwent a "spiritual transformation," in which he was purged of "the slightly arrogant attitude" he had occasionally shown before. She now found him "completely warm-hearted," and felt that "he understood the problems of people in trouble." There is a further conclusion, drawn by some fabricators of the legend, that he read widely and studied deeply during his illness and developed a firm social outlook that aligned him forever with the underprivileged. This notion is not sustained by Roosevelt's history during the prosperity of the 1920's. His human capacity, enlarged though it probably was, was not crystallized in either a new philosophy or a heightened interest in reforms.

For anyone of Roosevelt's background and character to have turned to serious social study or unorthodox political views would have been most unusual. From boyhood to the time of his illness he had led an outdoor athletic life, spending his indoor leisure on such diversions as stamp collections, ship models, naval history, and the like, not on sociological literature. His way of thinking was empirical, impressionistic, and pragmatic. At the beginning of his career he took to the patrician reform thought of the Progressive era and accepted a social outlook that can best be summed up in the phrase *noblesse oblige*.[1] He had a penchant for public service, personal philanthropy, and harmless manifestoes against dishonesty in government; he displayed a broad, easygoing tolerance, a genuine liking for all sorts of people; he loved to exercise his charm in political and social situations. His mind, as exhibited in writings and speeches of the twenties, was generous and sensible, but also superficial and complacent.

Roosevelt's education in politics came in a period of progressive optimism when it was commonly assumed that the most glaring ills of society could be cured by laws, once politics fell into the hands of honest men. If women worked endless hours in sweatshops, if workingmen were haunted by fear of unemployment or stricken by accidents, if the aged were beset by insecurity, men of good will would pass laws to help them. As a state Senator and as Governor this was what Roosevelt tried to do. But the social legislation of the states, however humane and useful, was worked out in provincial theaters of action, dealt more with effects than causes, touched only the surface of great problems like unemployment, housing, taxation, banking, and relief for agriculture. The generation that sponsored these laws got from them a good deal of training in practical politics and welfare work, but no strong challenge to think through the organic ills of society.

Roosevelt's biographers have largely ignored his life in the twenties except his fight for physical recovery, his role as peacemaker in the faction-ridden Democratic Party, and his return to politics as Governor of New York. John T. Flynn, however, has pointed with malicious pleasure to his unsuccessful career in business, which certainly deserves attention,

---

[1] "Frankness, and largeness, and simplicity, and a fine fervor for the right are virtues that some must preserve, and where can we look for them if not from the Roosevelts and the Delanos?" wrote Franklin K. Lane to Roosevelt, August, 1920. (Hofstadter footnote.)

not as a reflection on his ethics or personal capacities, but on his social views during the years of prosperity. The ventures with which Roosevelt was associated—chiefly, one suspects, for the promotional value of his name—were highly speculative, and with one exception they failed. Perhaps the most illuminating of these was the Consolidated Automatic Merchandising Corporation, of which he was a founder and director along with Henry Morgenthau, Jr. This was a holding company, whose promoters were stirred by the typically American idea of a chain of clerk-less stores to sell standard goods by means of automatic vending machines. In 1928 the chairman of its board announced that a large store staffed with such machines would soon be opened in New York City. Although it promised fabulous returns to investors, the firm lost over two million dollars within three years and closed its affairs in a bankruptcy court. Since Roosevelt promptly resigned his interest when he became Governor, his connection with it was brief and, in a business way, unimportant; but the social implications of the clerkless store and the jobless clerk, not to mention the loose and speculative way in which the enterprise was launched, do not seem to have troubled his mind.

In 1922 Roosevelt became president of the American Construction Council, a trade organization of the building industry. The council had been conceived in the light of Secretary of Commerce Hoover's philosophy of self-regulation by business, and Hoover presided over the meeting at which Roosevelt was chosen. In his address to the council Roosevelt endorsed the Hoover doctrine:

> The tendency lately has been toward regulation of industry. Something goes wrong somewhere in a given branch of work, immediately the public is aroused, the press, the pulpit and public call for an investigation. That is fine, that is healthy . . . but government regulation is not feasible. It is unwieldy, expensive. It means employment of men to carry on this phase of work; it means higher taxes. The public doesn't want it; the industry doesn't want it.

Seven years later in a Fourth of July speech at Tammany Hall, Governor Roosevelt warned of dangers inherent in "great combinations of capital." But he explained that "industrial combination is not wrong in itself. The danger lies in taking the government into partnership." The chief theme of his address was summed up in the sentence: "I want to preach a new doctrine—complete separation of business and government"—which was an ironic message for the future architect of the New Deal.

Even Mr. Flynn concedes that as Governor Roosevelt was "a fair executive." On social justice and humane reform his record was strong; in matters of long-range economic understanding and responsibility it was weak. He worked earnestly and effectively with a hostile Republican legislature to extend reforms that had been started by Al Smith. He secured a program of old-age pensions, unemployment insurance, and labor legislation, developed a forthright liberal program on the power question, and took the initiative in calling a conference of governors of Eastern industrial states to discuss unemployment and relief. His state was in the vanguard of those taking practical steps to relieve distress.

Along with most other Americans, however, Roosevelt had failed to foresee the depression that began when he was Governor. Six months before the crash he found New York industry "in a very healthy and prosperous condition." In his addresses and messages he ignored the significance of the depression until its effects became overwhelming. His signal failure was in the realm of financial policy.

On December 11, 1930 the Bank of United States in New York City was closed by the State Superintendent of Banks, in substantial default to 400,000 depositors, mostly people with small savings. It had long been a practice of some New York commercial banks to create special "thrift accounts," which, although much the same as ordinary savings accounts, stood outside the control of state laws regulating savings-bank investments and gave bankers a wide latitude with other people's money. Another device was to create bank affiliates which were manipulated in sundry complicated ways to milk depositors and stockholders for the benefit of insiders.

A few months before the collapse of the Bank of United States, the failure of the City Trust Company had led to an investigation of the State Banking Department, and in Roosevelt's absence Acting Governor Herbert Lehman appointed Robert Moses as investigator. Moses's report roundly condemned many bank practices, especially "thrift accounts" and bank affiliates, and referred to the Bank of United States as an especially flagrant case.

Roosevelt ignored the Moses report and created another commission to study the same subject, appointing as one of its members Henry Pollack—a director and counsel of the Bank of United States! Not surprisingly, the new commission rejected Moses's recommendations. Shortly afterward, when the Bank of United States failed, Roosevelt was self-assured, unabashed, impenitent. To the state legislature he boldly wrote: "The responsibility for strengthening the banking laws rests with you." Insisting that the protection of the laws be extended to depositors in thrift accounts, he waxed righteously impatient: "The people of the State not only expect it, but they have a right to demand it. The time to act is now. Any further delay is inexcusable. . . ."

This incident, particularly Roosevelt's sudden espousal of a reform he had opposed, foreshadows a great part of the history of the New Deal. There is an irresistible footnote to it. When Roosevelt came to power the banks of the nation were in paralysis. In his first press conference he was asked if he favored federal insurance of bank deposits. He said that he did not. His reason was that bad banks as well as good ones would have to be insured and that the federal government would have to take the losses. Nevertheless the Federal Deposit Insurance Corporation was soon created as a concession to a bloc of insistent Western Senators. The FDIC thus took its place among a company of New Deal reforms that add to the lustre of Roosevelt's name and will presumably be cited by historians as instances of his wise planning.

When the task of conducting a presidential campaign fell upon him, Roosevelt's background of economic innocence was dappled by only occasional traces of knowledge. "I don't find that he has read much about economic subjects," wrote Raymond Moley in a family letter, April 12, 1932. "The frightening aspect of his methods is FDR's great receptivity. So far as I know he makes no efforts to check up on anything that I or anyone else has told him." On occasion his advisers were astounded by his glib treatment of complicated subjects. Once when his campaign speeches on the tariff were being prepared, and two utterly incompatible proposals were placed before him, Roosevelt left Moley speechless by airily suggesting that he should "weave the two together." That "great receptivity" which frightened Moley, however, was the secret of Roosevelt's political genius. He became an individual sounding-board for the grievances and remedies of the nation, which he tried to weave into a program that would be politically, if not economically, coherent.

Roosevelt's 1932 campaign utterances indicate that the New Deal had not yet taken form in his mind. He was clear on two premises: he rejected Hoover's thesis that the depression began abroad, insisting that it was a home-made product, and he denounced Hoover for spending too much money. He called the Hoover administration "the greatest spending Administration in peace time in all our history." The current deficit, he charged, was enough to "make us catch our breath." "Let us have the courage," he urged, "to stop borrowing to meet continuing deficits." And yet he was "unwilling that economy should be practiced at the expense of starving people." Still, he did not indicate how he proposed to relieve starving people. Public works? They could be no more than a "stopgap," even if billions of dollars were spent on them. He was firm in ascribing the depression to low domestic purchasing power, and declared that the government must "use wise measures of regulation which will bring the purchasing power back to normal." On the other hand, he surrendered to Hoover's idea that America's productive capacity demanded a large outlet in the export market. "If our factories run even 80 percent of capacity," he said (quite inaccurately),[2] "they will turn out more products than we as a nation can possibly use ourselves. The answer is that . . . we must sell some goods abroad."

Roosevelt made several specific promises to the farmers. There was one aspect of Hoover's farm policies that made him especially bitter—the attempt of the Farm Board to organize *retrenchment* in production, which Roosevelt called "the cruel joke of advising farmers to allow twenty percent of their wheat lands to lie idle, to plow up every third row of cotton and shoot every tenth dairy cow." His own program involved "planned use of the land," reforestation, and aid to farmers by reducing tariffs through bilateral negotiations. Later he backtracked on the tariff, however, promising "continued protection for American agriculture *as well as* American industry."

All Roosevelt's promises—to restore purchasing power and mass employment and relieve the needy and aid the farmer and raise agricultural prices and balance the budget and lower the tariff and continue protection—added up to a very discouraging performance to those who hoped for a coherent liberal program. The *New Republic* called the campaign "an obscene spectacle" on both sides.

Roosevelt delivered one speech at the Commonwealth Club in San Francisco, however, which did generally foreshadow the new tack that was to be taken under the New Deal. In this address Roosevelt clearly set down the thesis that the nation had arrived at a great watershed in its development. Popular government and a wide continent to exploit had given the United States an unusually favored early history, he asserted. Then the Industrial Revolution had brought a promise of abundance for all. But its productive capacity had been controlled by ruthless and wasteful men. Possessing free land and a growing population, and needing industrial plant, the country had been willing to pay the price of the accomplishments of the "ambitious man" and had offered him "unlimited reward provided only that he produced the economic plant so

---

[2] " 'The United States,' concluded the authors of *America's Capacity to Consume*, 'has not reached a stage of economic development in which it is possible to produce more than the American people as a whole would like to consume.' " (Hofstadter footnote.)

much desired." "The turn of the tide came with the turn of the century."
As America reached its last frontiers, the demand of the people for more
positive controls of economic life gave rise to the Square Deal of Theodore Roosevelt and the New Freedom of Woodrow Wilson. In 1932
the nation was still faced with the problem of industrial control. . . .

In cold terms, American capitalism had come of age, the great era of
individualism, expansion, and opportunity was dead. Further, the drying
up of "natural" economic forces required that the government step in
and guide the creation of a new economic order. Thus far Roosevelt had
left behind the philosophy of his 1929 Tammany Hall speech. But in the
Commonwealth Club speech two different and potentially inconsistent
lines of government action are implied. One is suggested by the observation that the industrial plant is "overbuilt," that more plants will be "a
danger," that production must be "adjusted" to consumption; the other
by phrases like "meeting the problem of underconsumption," making
prosperity "uniform," distributing purchasing power, and "an economic
declaration of rights." The first involves a retrogressive economy of trade
restriction and state-guided monopoly; the second emphasizes social justice and the conquest of poverty. In 1931 the United States Chamber of
Commerce's Committee on Continuity of Business and Employment had
declared in terms similar to Roosevelt's: "A freedom of action which
might have been justified in the relatively simple life of the last century
cannot be tolerated today. . . . We have left the period of extreme individualism." The committee then proposed a program very closely re-
sembling the NRA as it was adopted in 1933. It is evident that Roosevelt's premises, far from being intrinsically progressive, were capable of
being adapted to very conservative purposes. His version of the "matured
economy" theory, although clothed in the rhetoric of liberalism and "social planning," could easily be put to the purposes of the trade associa-
tions and scarcity-mongers. The polar opposition between such a policy
and the promise of making prosperity uniform and distributing purchasing power anticipated a basic ambiguity in the New Deal.

At one of his earliest press conferences Roosevelt compared himself to
the quarterback in a football game. The quarterback knows what the
next play will be, but beyond that he cannot predict or plan too rigidly
because "future plays will depend on how the next one works." It was
a token of his cast of mind that he used the metaphor of a game, and one
in which chance plays a very large part. The New Deal will never be
understood by anyone who looks for a single thread of policy, a far-reaching, far-seeing plan. It was a series of improvisations, many adopted very

suddenly, many contradictory. Such unity as it had was in political strategy, not economics. . . .[3]

Roosevelt's admirers, their minds fixed on the image of a wise, benevolent, provident father, have portrayed him as an *ardent social reformer* and sometimes as a *master planner.* His critics, coldly examining the step-by-step emergence of his measures, studying the supremely haphazard way in which they were so often administered, finding how little he actually had to do with so many of his "achievements," have come to the opposite conclusion that his successes were purely accidental, just as a certain portion of a number of random shots is likely to hit a target. It is true, it is bound to be true, that there is a vast disproportion between Roosevelt's personal stature and the Roosevelt legend, but not everything that comes in haphazard fashion is necessarily an accident. During his presidential period the nation was confronted with a completely novel situation for which the traditional, commonly accepted philosophies afforded no guide. An era of fumbling and muddling-through was inevitable. Only a leader with an experimental temper could have made the New Deal possible.[4]

JAMES M. BURNS: A "POWER BROKER"

Another critical and suggestive appraisal of FDR's goals has been made by James M. Burns, a political scientist. Burns is concerned with the President's lack of an ideology, and his fascination with the manipulation of political power. He concludes that if at times such an attitude led FDR to constructive achievements, on other occasions it could lead him into irresponsibility.

During the first half of his first term Roosevelt tried a Grand Experiment in government. He took the role of national father, of bipartisan leader, of President of all the people. Playing this role with consummate skill, he extracted from it the last morsel of political power and government action. Eventually his biparty leadership was to falter, and he would turn in new directions. But during these first two years, 1933 and 1934, he savored the heady feeling of rising above parties and groups and acting almost as a constitutional monarch armed with political power.

---

[3] Richard Hofstadter, *The American Political Tradition and the Men Who Made It* (New York, 1954), pp. 318-327.
[4] *Ibid.,* p. 313.

The New Deal, the President told a Wisconsin crowd in August 1934, "seeks to cement our society, rich and poor, manual worker and brain worker, into a voluntary brotherhood of freemen, standing together, striving together, for the common good of all." Such government would not hurt honest business, he said; in seeking social justice it would not rob Peter to pay Paul. Government, he told a convention of bankers two months later, was "essentially the outward expression of the unity and leadership of all groups." His own role as president? It was "to find among many discordant elements that unity of purpose that is best for the Nation as a whole." Throughout Roosevelt's speeches of 1934 ran this theme of government as conciliator, harmonizer, unifier of all major interests. He was the master broker among the many interests of a great and diverse people.

As president of all the people Roosevelt tried to stay above the political and ideological battles that raged all around him. Insisting that he did not want to be drawn into controversy, he asked his supporters to take over the burden of answering attacks on the New Deal from the extreme right or left. He was forever acting as umpire between warring administrators or congressmen. When his advisers differed over policy he time and again ordered: "Put them in a room together, and tell them no lunch until they agree!" When Tugwell and Senator Copeland were at swords' points over food and drug legislation, the President suggested that they battle it out together while he sat in and held the sponge. He told his agency chiefs that he was operating between the 15 per cent on the extreme left and the 15 per cent on the extreme right who were opposing him for political reasons or "from pure cussedness." He insisted that he was going neither right nor left—just down the middle.

The country enjoyed a brief era of good feelings, and presiding jauntily over the era was Roosevelt himself. While the New Deal came in for some sharp criticism, everybody, it seemed, loved the President. William Randolph Hearst was a guest at the White House. The Scripps-Howard newspapers lauded his New Deal. Pierre Du Pont and other businessmen wrote him friendly letters. Farm leaders rallied to the cause. "To us," wrote Ed O'Neal of the American Farm Bureau Federation, "you are the Andrew Jackson of the Twentieth Century, championing the rights of the people. . . ." Father Coughlin defended him. William Green and other leaders of labor had little but words of praise for the man in the White House. Across the seas a man who seemed to love nobody had a good word for him. "I have sympathy with President Roosevelt," remarked Adolf Hitler in mid-1933, "because he marches straight to his objective over Congress, over lobbies, over stubborn bureaucracies."

Some Democrats could not understand Roosevelt's nonpartisan line. When one of them naïvely suggested early in 1934 that the President come to a celebration for the Democratic party's patron saint, the President gently rebuked him. He would take no part in Jefferson Day celebrations that year: "Our strongest plea to the country in this particular year of grace," he said, "is that the recovery and reconstruction program is being accomplished by men and women of all parties—that I have repeatedly appealed to Republicans as much as to Democrats to do their part." Much as he loved Jefferson, it would be better if "nonpartisan Jefferson dinners" should be held, with as many Republicans as Democrats on the banquet committees. He made no objection to a nationwide tribute to himself on the occasion of his birthday, in the interest of crippled children.

Republican party leaders were perplexed too. During the first months they were content to mute their protests and to bask in the patriotic posture of "country before party." But slowly the party emerged from its torpor. Its task was formidable at best. Republican leadership had been decimated in two national elections. Living almost in oblivion, Hoover was a scapegoat even for his own party, and the Republican leaders in Congress seemed pedestrian and heavy-footed next to the lustrous, fast-moving figure in the White House. By early 1934 they were trying hard to act as a real opposition party.

But what were they to oppose? A cardinal aspect of Roosevelt's nonpartisanship was his quarterbacking now on the right, now on the left, now down the center of the political field. As in the 1932 campaign, he did not leave an opening at either end of his line through which the Republicans could try to carry the ball. Indeed, the Grand Old Party itself tended to split into factions to the right and to the left of the President's erratic middle-of-the-road course. Despite their minority position in the party, the progressive Republicans like Norris and McNary had the advantage of White House smiles and favors.

A remarkable aspect of this situation was that Roosevelt continued in 1934 to take a more moderate and conservative stand on policy than did the majority of congressmen. On silver, on inflation, on mortgage refinancing, on labor, on spending, Congress was to the left of the President. In contrast with later periods, Roosevelt's main job in 1933 and 1934 was not to prod Congress into action, but to ride the congressional whirlwind by disarming the extremists, by seeking unity among the blocs, and by using every presidential weapon of persuasion and power.

The classic test of greatness in the White House has been the chief executive's capacity to lead Congress. Weak presidents have been those

who had no program to offer, or whose proposals have been bled away
in the endless twistings and windings of the legislative process. Strong
presidents have been those who finessed or bulldozed their programs
through Congress and wrote them into legislative history. By this classic
test Roosevelt—during his first years in the White House—was a strong
President who dominated Congress with a masterly show of leadership.

If Roosevelt had ever stopped during these turbulent days to list his
methods of dealing with Congress, the result might have looked something like this:

1. Full use of constitutional powers, such as the veto
2. Good timing
3. Drafting of measures in the executive branch
4. Almost constant pressure, adroitly applied
5. Careful handling of patronage
6. Face-to-face persuasiveness with legislative leaders
7. Appeal to the people.

But it would have been out of character for the President to catalogue
his methods in such systematic fashion. He cheerfully played the legislative game by ear, now trying this device and now that, as the situation
dictated.

He experimented even with a policy of hands off for a short period.
Late in March 1934 the President ostentatiously left Washington for two
weeks of deep-sea fishing off the Bahamas. White House pressure was
relaxed. Soon Congress was looking like a schoolroom of disorderly boys
with the master gone. A wrangle broke out among Democrats over regulation of stock exchanges. Over one hundred representatives, breaking
away from their leaders, lined up in favor of a mortgage refinancing bill
so inflationary that Roosevelt sent word to Garner and Rayburn from
his yacht to tell Congress "if this type of wild legislation passed the
responsibility for wrecking recovery will be squarely on the Congress, and
I will not hesitate to say so to the nation in plain language." Garner
said that in thirty years he had never seen the House in such abject tur-
moil.

The hands-off experiment was a dismal failure. Welcomed by a group
of congressmen on his return Roosevelt remarked pointedly that he had
learned some lessons from the barracuda and sharks. He added with a
smile, "I am a tough guy."

The presidential reins were tightened, but the President never got
really tough. He depended mainly on conferences with congressional

leaders to put across his program. He even denied that there was such a thing as "must legislation."

"The word 'must' is a terrible word," he told reporters. "I would not use 'must' to Congress. I never have, have I?" he finished amid laughter.

His formal constitutional powers in legislation Roosevelt exploited to the hilt. Reviving Wilson's practice, he delivered his reports on the state of the union to Congress in person. He outlined general proposals in well-timed messages, and he followed these up by detailed legislative proposals drafted in the executive departments and introduced by friendly congressmen. Individual legislators were drawn into the executive policymaking process not as representatives of Congress nor their constituencies, but as members of the administration. The President met frequently with congressional leaders and committee chairmen, and occasionally with other members of Congress. In practice he fashioned a kind of "master-ministry" of bureaucrats and congressmen with Roosevelt at the top.

The President could say no, too. During his first two years he used his veto powers to a far greater extent than the average of all the previous presidents. Many of the vetoed bills involved special legislation, which Roosevelt had his assistants scrutinize carefully. More important than the veto was the President's threat to use it. Again and again he sent word through congressional leaders that he would turn down a pending bill unless it was changed. On one occasion in 1934, when Congress passed an immigration bill that seemed to Roosevelt filled with inequities, he simply proposed that the two Houses pass a concurrent resolution of recall—otherwise he would veto the bill. Only once did the Seventy-third Congress override Roosevelt; this occasion followed a legislative revolt against the President's economy program.

Roosevelt played the patronage game tirelessly and adroitly. Major appointments were allotted on the basis of lists the President drew up of "our friends" in various states; an opponent he carefully designated simply as "not with me." Routine jobs he turned over to Farley. Thousands of applicants besieged Farley in his office and hotel until the Postmaster General had to sneak back and forth to his office as if he were dodging a sheriff's writ. Farley flouted custom by openly accepting and systematizing patronage procedures. When his outer office became packed, he calmly went about the room followed by a stenographer taking the name of each person and the kind of job he wanted. Only because the new emergency agencies were hiring employees outside the classified civil service (about a hundred thousand such jobs by July 1934) was Farley able to take care of the host of deserving Democrats.

Congressmen wanted jobs too, and the President saw that they got them. When a delegation of Democratic representatives complained to him about the treatment they had got on patronage from departments, he promptly asked the cabinet to be as helpful as possible with congressmen on this matter. The President was shrewd enough, however, to postpone job distribution during the first session long enough to apply the test of administration support, with the result, it was said, that "his relations with Congress were to the end of the session tinged with a shade of expectancy which is the best part of young love."

Roosevelt was not above back-alley horse trades. In the spring of 1934 Senator "Cotton Ed" Smith of South Carolina pigeonholed the Chief Executive's nomination of Tugwell as Under Secretary of Agriculture. But Smith also badly wanted a United States marshalship for a henchman who had a good reputation except for a slight case of homicide. So Roosevelt made the deal, and greeted an astonished Tugwell with the cheery remark: "You will never know any more about it, I hope; but today I traded you for a couple of murderers!"

Roosevelt often fell back on his own charm and resourcefulness in dealing with congressmen. Ickes watched in admiration one day as the President handled a ticklish problem of patronage. Senate Majority Leader Robinson was insisting on the appointment as commissioner of Indian affairs of a man whom Ickes felt to be totally disqualified. When an ugly row seemed in the offing, the President had the two antagonists to tea. First he established a friendly atmosphere by discussing with Robinson a number of pending bills that the President and Senator both favored. Then he let Robinson and Ickes briefly make their cases about the appointment. Before an argument could develop, the President turned the subject back to general policies. When dinner was announced, Roosevelt said pleasantly to Robinson, "Well, Joe, you see what I am up against. . . ." Robinson replied that there was nothing further he could say, and left. Even so, the President waited a day or two, and then sent in the name of another man.

Roosevelt was a genius at placating his bickering lieutenants. Ickes was a chronic grumbler, staying after cabinet sessions to pour out his troubles. Sometimes harassed officials, feeling that their chief had forgotten them, used the threat of resigning as a means of getting their way—or, at the least, of getting attention from the White House. The President bore these pinpricks with marvelous good humor. But he knew how to teach a lesson too. Once when he heard that an important administrator was about to resign he telephoned him: "I have just had some bad news, Don. Secretary Hull is threatening to resign. He is very angry because I don't agree with him that we ought to remove the Ambassador to Kamchatka and make him third secretary to the Embassy at Svodia." Quickly catching on, the official agreed that his threat to resign was very foolish indeed.

Roosevelt's way with the press also showed his mastery of the art of government. He made so much news and maintained such a friendly attitude toward the newspapermen covering the White House that he quickly and easily won their sympathy. The newspapermen were especially pleased that the President had reinstituted the press conference, thus enabling them to question him directly. No one knew better than Roosevelt, however, that the press conference was a two-edged sword: he could use it to gain a better press, but the reporters could also use it to trip him. Much depended on knowing when *not* to answer a question.

One day, while instructing his agency chiefs on public relations, Roosevelt told them how he had handled an awkward query. A reporter had asked him to comment on a statement by Ambassador Bingham in London urging closer relations between the United States and Britain. If he had done the natural thing of backing up Bingham, the newspapers would have made headlines of the President's statement, with likely ill effect on naval conversations then under way with Japan. If he had said "no comment," he would have sounded critical of Bingham's statement. So he simply said he had not seen it—although in fact he had.

Roosevelt used his most tactical weapons for dealing with Congress. "The coming session will be comparatively easy to handle," Roosevelt wrote to Colonel House in December 1933, "though it may not be noiseless." The President did not make the near-perfect score in this session that he had the year before, but he got through most of his program and staved off bills he disliked. To Hull's infinite satisfaction Congress passed the Reciprocal Tariff Act as an emergency measure to stimulate foreign trade without disturbing any "sound" or "important" American interest, as the President put it. The Gold Reserve Act was passed in virtually the form Roosevelt had asked; he hailed it as a decisive step by which the government took firmly in its own hands control of the gold value of the dollar. Farm benefits were extended to growers of cotton, tobacco, and other commodities. The President's requests for stock exchange regulation and for two billions in bonds for refinancing farm mortgages were converted into legislation.

On other issues, however, the outcome was different. Roosevelt had to negotiate with the silver bloc for weeks before reaching a bargain under which the Treasury would purchase heavy amounts of silver and thus shore up the domestic silver market. On a clear-cut sectional issue, the St. Lawrence Waterway Treaty, the President met defeat, with Democratic senators from states supposedly hurt by the waterway voting against the treaty and killing it. And both chambers by sweeping majorities overrode a presidential veto of an appropriations bill that would have restored part of Roosevelt's pay cut for government employees.

When Congress could not interfere, Roosevelt acted with decision. Constitutionally the President had exclusive power to grant or withhold recognition of foreign governments. On November 17, 1933, Roosevelt announced the resumption of diplomatic relations between the United States and the Soviet Union. This action came after lengthy haggling over terms. Moscow promised to refrain from abetting revolutionary activity against the American political or social order, and to protect the right of free religious worship of Americans in Russia. Rosy plans were laid for expansion of trade between the two nations. Although some of the President's friends (and his mother) opposed recognition, the action seemed to be well received by most Americans, including many businessmen and Republicans.

Many measures passed by Congress granted sweeping powers to the President. By the close of the Seventy-third Congress he held unprecedented controls over a peacetime American economy. Yet Roosevelt did not seek all the power he got. In several instances Congress granted him wide discretion, simply because the factions on Capitol Hill split wide open on thorny political matters and could agree only on leaving final decision with the White House. This was true of farm relief, the NRA, and the tariff. Power, it is said, goes to the power-seeking, but in these cases it was also the temper of the times and the divisions in Congress that enlarged presidential power.

The Roosevelt technique with Congress dazzled the country; but there were misgivings. One of those who was not enchanted was a keen student of national politics at Harvard named E. Pendleton Herring. Analyzing the first two sessions of Roosevelt's Congress, Herring noted the extent to which presidential control had rested on unsteady bases such as patronage, government funds and favors, the co-operation of congressional leaders, and the crisis psychology of the people. Even so, Herring noted, the administration could do little more than "keep order in the breadline that reached into the Treasury." The more powerfully organized groups got much of what they wanted; the weaker groups, such as labor and consumers, did not do so well. The President had shown himself as an astute politician rather than a crusader. Responsible executive leadership seemed weak in the face of organized minorities.

"Can the presidential system," asked Herring, "continue as a game of touch and go between the Chief Executive and congressional *blocs* played by procedural dodges and with bread and circuses for forfeits?"

It was a good question—but the American people in 1933 and 1934 were more concerned with "bread and circuses" than with academic anxieties.[5]

ARTHUR M. SCHLESINGER, JR.: FDR, JEFFERSONIAN LIBERAL

A more favorable estimate than that of Hofstadter or Burns is provided by Arthur M. Schlesinger, Jr., author of the multi-volume masterpiece, The Age of Roosevelt. *In analyzing important strands in FDR's character, Schlesinger emphasizes his pragmatic attitude, his humanity, or genuine sympathy for people, and his energetic use of executive powers as provided by the Constitution. Like FDR himself, he views the New Deal as utilizing Hamiltonian powers to implement Jeffersonian ends.*

For Roosevelt, the technique of liberal government was pragmatism. Tugwell talked about creating "a philosophy to fit the Rooseveltian method"; but this was the aspiration of an intellectual. Nothing attracted Roosevelt less than rigid intellectual systems. "The fluidity of change in society has always been the despair of theorists," Tugwell once wrote. This fluidity was Roosevelt's delight, and he floated upon it with the confidence of an expert sailor, who could detect currents and breezes invisible to others, hear the slap of waves on distant rocks, smell squalls beyond the horizon and make infallible landfalls in the blackest of fogs. He respected clear ideas, accepted them, employed them, but was never really at ease with them and always ultimately skeptical about their relationship to reality.

His attitude toward economists was typical. Though he acknowledged their necessity, he stood in little awe of them. "I brought down several books by English economists and leading American economists," he once told a press conference. ". . . I suppose I must have read different articles by fifteen different experts. Two things stand out: The first is that no two of them agree, and the other thing is that they are so foggy in what they say that it is almost impossible to figure out what they mean. It is jargon; absolute jargon." Once Roosevelt remarked to Keynes of Leon Henderson, "Just look at Leon. When I got him, he was only an econo-

[5] James M. Burns, *Roosevelt: The Lion and the Fox* (New York, 1956), pp. 183-191.

mist." (Keynes could hardly wait to repeat this to Henderson.) Roosevelt dealt proficiently with practical questions of government finance, as he showed in his press conferences on the budget; but abstract theory left him cold.

Considering the state of economic theory in the nineteen thirties, this was not necessarily a disabling prejudice. Roosevelt had, as J. K. Galbraith has suggested, what was more important than theory, and surely far more useful than bad theory, a set of intelligent economic attitudes. He believed in government as an instrument for effecting economic change (though not as an instrument for doing everything: in 1934, he complained to the National Emergency Council, "There is the general feeling that it is up to the Government to take care of everybody . . . they should be told all the different things the Government can not do"). He did not regard successful businessmen as infallible repositories of economic wisdom. He regarded the nation as an estate to be improved for those who would eventually inherit it. He was willing to try nearly anything. And he had a sense of the complex continuities of history—that special intimacy with the American past which, as Frances Perkins perceptively observed, signified a man who had talked with old people who had talked with older people who remembered many things back to the War of the Revolution.

From this perspective, Roosevelt could not get excited about the debate between the First and Second New Deals. No one knew what he really thought about the question of the organic economy versus the restoration of competition. Tugwell, perhaps the most vigilant student of Roosevelt's economic ideas, could in one mood pronounce Roosevelt "a progressive of the nineteenth century in economic matters" (1946) who "clung to the Brandeis-Frankfurter view" (1950) and "could be persuaded away from the old progressive line only in the direst circumstances" (1950); in another, he could speak of Roosevelt's "preference for a planned and disciplined business system" (1957) and for "overhead management of the whole economy" (1940), and question whether he ever believed in Brandeis (1957). Corcoran and Cohen, who helped persuade Roosevelt to the Second New Deal, thought he never really abandoned the NRA dream of directing the economy through some kind of central economic mechanism. Roosevelt himself, confronted with a direct question, always wriggled away ("Brandeis is one thousand per cent right in principle but in certain fields there must be a guiding or restraining hand of Government because of the very nature of the specific field"). He never could see why the United States has to be all one way or all the other. "This country is big enough to experiment with several diverse systems and follow several different lines," he once remarked to Adolf Berle. "Why must we put our economic policy in a single systemic strait jacket?"

Rejecting the battle between the New Nationalism and the New Freedom which had so long divided American liberalism, Roosevelt equably defined the New Deal as the "satisfactory combination" of both. Rejecting the platonic distinction between "capitalism" and "socialism," he led the way toward a new society which took elements from each and rendered both obsolescent. It was this freedom from dogma which outraged the angry, logical men who saw everything with dazzling certitude. Roosevelt's illusion, said Herbert Hoover, was "that any economic system would work in a mixture of others. No greater illusions ever mesmerized the American people." "Your President," said Leon Trotsky with contempt, "abhors 'systems' and 'generalities.' . . . Your philosophic method is even more antiquated than your economic system." But the American President always resisted ideological commitment. His determination was to keep options open within the general frame of a humanized democracy; and his belief was that the very diversity of systems strengthened the basis for freedom.

Without some critical vision, pragmatism could be a meaningless technique; the flight from ideology, a form of laziness; the middle way, an empty conception. For some politicians, such an approach meant nothing more than splitting the difference between extremes; the middle of the road was thus determined by the clamor from each side. At times it appeared to mean little more than this to Roosevelt. But at bottom he had a guiding vision with substantive content of its own. The content was not, however, intellectual; and this was where he disappointed more precise and exacting minds around him. It was rather a human content, a sense of the fortune and happiness of people. In 1936 a Canadian editor asked him to state his objectives. Roosevelt's off-the-cuff reply defined his goal in all its naïveté and power:

> . . . to do what any honest Government of any country would do; try to increase the security and the happiness of a larger number of people in all occupations of life and in all parts of the country; to give them more of the good things of life, to give them a greater distribution not only of wealth in the narrow terms, but of wealth in the wider terms; to give them places to go in the summer time—recreation; to give them assurance that they are not going to starve in their old age; to give honest business a chance to go ahead and make a reasonable profit, and to give everyone a chance to earn a living.

The listing was neither considered nor comprehensive, but the spirit was accurate. "The intellectual and spiritual climate," said Frances Perkins, "was Roosevelt's general attitude that *the people mattered.*" Nothing else would count until ordinary people were provided an environment and an opportunity "as good as human ingenuity can devise and fit for children of God."

Developed against the backdrop of depression, his philosophy of compassion had a particular bias toward the idea of security—"a greater physical and mental and spiritual security for the people of this country." "Security," he once said,

> means a kind of feeling within our individual selves that we have lacked all through the course of history. We have had to take our chance about our old age in days past. We have had to take our chance with depressions and boom times. We have had to take chances on buying our homes. I have believed for a great many years that the time has come in our civilization when a great many of these chances should be eliminated from our lives.

The urgencies of depression carried the concern for security to a degree which later generations, who thought they could assume abundance and move on to problems of opportunity and self-fulfillment, would find hard to understand. The old American dream, Roosevelt told a collection of young people in 1935, was the dream of the golden ladder—each individual for himself. But the newer generation would have a different dream: "Your advancement, you hope, is along a broad highway on which thousands of your fellow men and women are advancing with you." In many ways this was a dispiriting hope. In the longer run, security, while indispensable as a social minimum, might be cloying and perhaps even stultifying as a social ideal.

But this was a nuance imposed by depression. His essential ideals had an old-fashioned flavor. He was unconsciously seeing America in the Jeffersonian image of Dutchess County and Hyde Park. He hoped, as he said, to extend "to our national life the old principal of the local community, the principle that no individual, man, woman, or child, has a right to do things that hurt his neighbors." "Our task of reconstruction does not require the creation of new and strange values. It is rather the finding of the way once more to known, but to some degree forgotten ideals." He wanted to make other people happy as he had been happy himself. Lifting his right hand high, his left hand only a little, he would say, "This difference is too big, it must become smaller—like this. . . . Wasn't I able to study, travel, take care of my sickness? The man who doesn't have to worry about his daily bread is securer and freer." He spoke of his philosophy as "social-mindedness." He meant by this essentially the humanization of industrial society.

A viewpoint so general provided no infallible guide to daily decision. Roosevelt therefore had to live by trial and error. His first term had its share of error: the overextension of NRA; the fumbling with monetary policy; the reluctant approach to spending; the waste of energy in trying to achieve the communitarian dream; the bungling of the London Economic Conference; the administrative confusion and conflict; the excessive reliance on ballyhoo and oratory. At times Roosevelt seemed almost to extemporize for the joy of it; his pragmatism appeared an addition to playing by ear in the nervous conviction that any kind of noise was better than silence. "Instead of being alarmed by the spirit of improvisation," wrote George Creel, "he seemed delighted by it, whooping on the improvisers with the excitement of one riding to hounds."

The chronic changing of front exposed the New Deal to repeated charges that it had no core of doctrine, that it was improvised and opportunistic, that it was guided only by circumstance. These charges were all true. But they also represented the New Deal's strength. For the advantage enjoyed by the pragmatists over the ideologists was their exceptional sensitivity to social and human reality. They measured results in terms not of conformity to a priori models but of concrete impact on people's lives. The New Deal thus had built-in mechanisms of feed-back, readjustment, and self-correction. Its incoherences were considerably more faithful to a highly complicated and shifting reality than any preconceived dogmatic system could have been. In the welter of confusion and ignorance, experiment corrected by compassion was the best answer.

Roosevelt's genius lay in the fact that he recognized—rather, rejoiced in—the challenge to the pragmatic nerve. His basic principle was not to sacrifice human beings to logic. Frances Perkins describes him as "in full revolt against the 'economic man.'" He had no philosophy save experiment, which was a technique; constitutionalism, which was a procedure; and humanity, which was a faith. . . .[6]

People wrote him because they saw him as a friend, deeply and personally responsive to their troubles. They cut his picture out of the paper, framed it in gilt cardboard and put it on their tables. When he spoke, they clustered around the radio, nodding in agreement and relief. Martha Gellhorn, writing from North Carolina in 1934, found the President's por-

[6] Arthur M. Schlesinger, Jr., [The Age of Roosevelt] The Politics of Upheaval (Boston, 1960), pp. 649-654.

trait in every house; he was "at once God and their intimate friend; he knows them all by name, knows their little town and mill, their little lives and problems. . . . He is there, and will not let them down." Lorena Hickok reported from New Orleans: "People down here all seem to think they know the President personally! . . . They feel he is talking to each one of them." They told her in Los Angeles: "He makes us all feel that he is talking directly to us as individuals." "I have heard him spoken of with an almost fanatical fervor," wrote Walter Davenport of *Collier's*. ". . . I have been where unemployed men have knocked down a possible employer who had sneered, 'Go ask your friend Roosevelt for a job.' " "More than any man who has been President within the memory of any of us now living," said Sherwood Anderson, "he has made us feel close to him."

Some, including a few who supported his policies, found the simplicities of the fireside chat a bit patronizing, even false. "There is a man leaning across his desk," John Dos Passos observed of the radio voice, "speaking clearly and cordially to youandme, explaining how he's sitting at his desk there in Washington, leaning towards youandme across his desk, speaking clearly and cordially so that youandme shall completely understand that he sits at his desk there in Washington with his fingers on all the switchboards of the federal government." But this was a sophisticated reaction. Most people thought the communication spontaneous and authentic. He came through to people because they felt—correctly—that he liked them and cared about them: one form of sentimentality reached out to another. Frances Perkins, watching him deliver a fireside chat, noted how unconscious he was of those around him at the White House as he concentrated on visualizing the plain folk listening at the other end. As he talked, his head would go up and down and his hands move in simple, natural gestures. "His face would smile and light up as though he were actually sitting on the front porch or in the parlor with them. People felt this, and it bound them to him in affection." They saw him primarily in personal terms, not only as strong and effective, but as warm and understanding, carrying an authority to which they were glad to submit and a humanity in which they felt total trust. And they saw him in addition as a gay and confident champion of their cause, a man who loved a fight and feared no one. As Westbrook Pegler remarked with surprise, Roosevelt had shown himself "a tremendously tough rough-and-tumble fighter, who will use any hitch that comes to mind, and expects to be used the same way." F.D.R. cared for the people, battled for them, and exulted in the battle.

It was the image of human warmth in a setting of dramatic national action which made people love him, not any special necromancy as a politician. Can the political art in any case be practiced apart from objectives? As a politician per se, Roosevelt has been overrated. While he worked hard and handled political problems with general skill and efficiency, he showed no evidence of supernatural talent. Any Democrat could have been elected President in 1932; given the New Deal, any Democrat stood a chance of election in 1936. In a later period, when the going got harder, Roosevelt would commit egregious political errors. It was not any technical wizardry as a politician but rather his brilliant dramatization of politics as the medium for education and leadership which accounted for his success. Beyond the backdrop of the depression and the deeds of the New Deal, Roosevelt gained his popular strength from that union of personality and public idealism which he joined so irresistibly to create so profoundly compelling a national image.[7]

o/the Roosevelt Leadership

E. E. ROBINSON: FDR, FAILURE OF LEADERSHIP

1955

> *One of the severest estimates of FDR's Presidency by a professional historian came from Professor E. E. Robinson of Stanford University, a former associate of Herbert Hoover. Robinson took FDR to task for his failure to provide leadership both at home and abroad. He castigated the confusion he suspected in FDR's mind, as well as FDR's ineffectiveness as an administrator of the New Deal. He found FDR's weaknesses in diplomacy especially disturbing—particularly his insistence on the unconditional surrender of Germany during World War II, and his failure to discern Soviet aims during the post-war era. In the light of more favorable appraisals of FDR, Robinson's strictures deserve consideration.*

Despite winning the war and maintaining the support of the American people, Franklin Roosevelt underwent the supreme tragedy of effective leadership. This tragedy lay not in the fact that death robbed him of triumph. The inexorable forces of time engulfed the world, revealing the basic weakness and long-enduring follies that existed among the American people he had served so long. The basic problems that the President had faced and for which he had offered solutions were still the problems of the American people.

In dealing with these problems in the decade following Mr. Roosevelt's death, American leaders of all shades of opinion and many degrees of un-

---

[7] Arthur M. Schlesinger, Jr., [*The Age of Roosevelt*] *The Coming of the New Deal* (Boston, 1959), pp. 571-573.

derstanding found that they had to contend with the continuing influence of the President upon the people. The majority of the electorate had voted for Roosevelt repeatedly, and a great many would go on voting the Roosevelt program for many years.

Such an assignment as was given him by the American people had been given no other. Seeking power and more power as a mode of self-expression—the dominant drive throughout his life—Franklin Roosevelt had taken to himself more power than any American had ever exercised.

From the outset he played the role in the grand manner. His physical handicap was in itself an aid. He was at the center of the stage. Most traveled of all rulers, wherever his plane or ship or car stopped, he became the focus of men's thoughts and emotions and actions. He was a mighty symbol of the United States of America.

If there were a throne in the modern world, here it was in all its grandeur. By personal inclination and by painstaking preparation, Franklin Roosevelt seemed to embody the powers of a man who had all the future for his own. However much the world outside the United States might recognize such a figure as familiar, nothing in the history of the United States—since the time when George Washington refused to have the attributes of a monarch or the title of King—had prepared the American people for this.

There is no escape from a fact repeatedly stated, yet often overlooked because of its utter familiarity: the ultimate authority, the American electorate, was responsible for Roosevelt's opportunity. His had been no arbitrary seizure of power, nor had duress been used in his elections. It was no contrived result that could later be proved false. Nor had illegal means been used in retaining his power. The people had said repeatedly: "Go forward as our representative in accordance with the programs and policies and objectives outlined."

Of course the tremendous reach of this Presidential rule had been possible because of the industrial and scientific might of the United States. This Mr. Roosevelt marshaled on behalf of the masses seeking to escape from the despotism of dictators. It was this mighty tribune of the people who authorized the experimentation and construction through which emerged the most destructive weapon in all history.

So far, indeed, had personal power asserted itself that President Roosevelt had within his grasp—as he neared the end—not only the creation of a structure for world peace, but the creation of a physical power that could destroy the world or build it in the image of an entirely new scientific perspective.

Buoyant, hopeful, zestful, eager, experimental, he had reflected the emotions that all youth felt and all who had passed youth remembered with either regret or misgiving—but usually with understanding. He dealt with the mass of mankind the world around, as he dealt with groups of his fellow countrymen, and as he was wont to deal with individuals who crowded about him.

Franklin Roosevelt saw himself in the role of a "happy warrior" even during the crises of his days of supremacy. And the American people—who in their lighter moments crave a hero in sport, on the stage, or in combat —saw in their President one who had triumphed over adversity, risen to great heights of personal achievement, and was mastering the forces of evil.

As politics for the majority of Americans had always been the favorite of all games, here, more nearly than ever before in their history, was a hero to match their dreams. He could "walk with Kings—nor lose the common touch," and had, in truth, "forced heart and nerve and sinew to serve his turn long after they [were] gone."

To the end, Franklin Roosevelt never left his class. He remained aloof in his feeling, his manner, his attitude. However much camaraderie existed, it was that of the leader relaxing with those who served him. His attitude in press conferences, his predilection for personal consultation with rulers of foreign nations, his superb confidence in dealing with political rivals—revealed that here was a man born to rule.

Dramatic were his repeated overtures to Hitler, to Mussolini, and later to Stalin. And these, in addition to his correspondence with other heads of states, were evidence of his use of the power of place to determine public policy, quite apart from the usual formal approaches through diplomatic representatives.

Franklin Roosevelt had a lively sense of his place in history. It could hardly have been otherwise. This had an important part in his ceaseless gathering of the materials bearing on his actions in public office. He expressed a view that must often have been in his mind when, in a tribute to Justice Oliver Wendell Holmes on the one hundredth anniversary of the birth of the Justice, he wrote: "It is the quality of great men that they continue to live long after they are gone."

What a man says himself is of great value, but it must be measured always by his comprehension, his outlook, and his purpose. It is here, perhaps, that we are on the surest ground in judging how great a leader Roosevelt was. Of his conception of the majesty and power of the Presidency, there is no question. It is written large in his utterances and in his attitude, certainty, and finality in action.

Of his deep comprehension of the basic problems of statecraft there is grave question. His simplicity in explanation of what seemed to him the fundamentals of economics and politics, of philosophy and of science, is the best evidence of his limitations. He was thoughtful and deeply aspiring, but singularly naïve, particularly about himself. Consequently his record as prepared and his explanations of events for "the future historian" are often superficial and must be judged as such in any analysis and judgment of his contributions.

Specialists trained in the law and in economics find it more difficult to explain Mr. Roosevelt's methods than specialists trained in politics. The reason is apparent in his own primary interest. But specialists in psychology and history find much that is enlightening in his procedures and in his declared objectives. Nearest, perhaps, to a full understanding of his method of action and his use of language are those whose primary interest is in biography. The abiding interest that held Mr. Roosevelt throughout the years was in human beings, and most of all in the human being whose life he knew best and whose life he wished biographers to understand in all the years to come.

The historian of these fateful years in the life of the American people must face the problem of evaluating the mind of Mr. Roosevelt. He must not be deterred from a conclusion by realization that he is formulating a concept for his own use that has not the certainty of scientific analysis or the finality of a judgment of God.

There is much evidence. Contemporaries supply it in abundance, and it must be added, without fundamental agreement. There is easy escape in the oft-asserted conclusion that the mind of the President was complex, baffling, and beyond comprehension. But this will not suffice.

Of all the evidence available to the historian, none ranks in importance with three sources: first, *F.D.R.: His Personal Letters,* particularly to friends; second, his speeches, especially those that are known to be his own; and third, his extemporaneous remarks which have been recorded. Of these, the extemporaneous remarks, particularly in press conferences, are most revealing of the mind that, in its power of decision and opportunity of evasion, governed the United States for more than a decade and determined in great measure the lives of all peoples in the world for a half-dozen years.

On the basis of an examination of these sources, it is a conclusion here stated that the mind was one of vivid imagination, amazing grasp of detail, but also of unusual confusion, of inconsistency, often given to down-right evasion. Explanation of his evasions and inconsistencies owing to the immensity of his task and the importance of keeping controls at all cost—does not change the fundamental conclusion.

A contemporary who watched as a close observer of the President throughout these years concluded that there was "absolutely no one who knew the President's mind." It was, he said, "Indolent, superficial, gay, deeply interested in the trivial—yet forced to deal with subjects and problems beyond its comprehension."

Perhaps as clear a reflection of the perplexity that Mr. Roosevelt caused even his most devoted supporters is to be found in *The Secret Diary of Harold L. Ickes*. It was "impossible to come to grips with him," wrote Mr. Ickes.

That the President's trait of seeming preoccupation with non-essentials —for whatever reason, deliberate or otherwise—intruded at important moments is admitted by Mr. Rosenman in his notes descriptive of the conference at Teheran, where Roosevelt was the moderator, arbitrator and final authority. "His contributions to the conversations," reports Rosenman, "were infrequent and sometimes annoyingly irrelevant, but it appears time and again—at Teheran and at Yalta—that it was he who spoke the last word."

Testimony upon Mr. Roosevelt as administrator is practically unanimous to the effect that he was not efficient or effective. A lesser man or one burdened with lesser tasks could have made exact, direct, meticulous, and neat decisions. But in his performance of his function as administrator, he had to delegate great powers of administration, and he should have delegated more.

His task, as he conceived of it, was one that compelled confusion, inconsistency and inconclusiveness—and this for an ever-present reason. To keep in working order personal advisers, Cabinet officers, Congressional leaders and the press, he had to be all things to all men. And he alone could be judge of the timing, the emergency, and the outcome. The task called for a consummate artist in the field of guessing. . . .

* * *

In interpreting Mr. Roosevelt's utterances, it has been shown repeatedly in the foregoing pages that there is need to determine not only the sources of the ideas expressed, but also the process by which the speech came to be "his own."

So, too, in the analysis of the great acts of his administration, it is obvious that there were innumerable cases, as has been shown, where the decision was definitely his own. But countless—and in some cases major—decisions were products of other men's determination and power. An understanding of Mr. Roosevelt's action must therefore be based upon knowledge of the work of his chosen advisers.

The innumerable advisers who had so large a part in the years of Franklin Roosevelt's administration were not "practical men." They were, in a very real sense, dreamers. Of course the dreamers carried with them many practical men. But the remedies and the plans for a "new world" were the work of men who did not always count the cost in money, men, or morale. As zealots—dedicated to great causes—they struck a responsive chord in the hearts of many of their fellow citizens.

An unusual combination of political forces brought to the dreamers great opportunities that were continued through the years, until they could dream not only for America, but for all mankind. This had much to do with bringing Americans into World War II and into the United Nations Organization. . . .

Franklin D. Roosevelt shaped the history of his country—and of the world—because he always appeared to be affirmative. He proclaimed the affirmative attitude to be all-important. To the American people in despondency after a period of disillusionment he had said we can and will succeed! To a world sunk in the despondency of long suffering, he had said we can build a better world! And the magic rested in the fact that speaking with such assurance of objectives and not of obstacles, he reflected precisely what his hearers wished to hear.

*　　*　　*

Roosevelt's leadership resulted in fundamental changes in the government itself: in tremendous concentration of power in the Executive; in building up a vast system of bureaucratic control of private business; and by adding direct economic support of the citizen to the careful adjustment of conflicting economic interests in a free enterprise system.

The revolution consisted in the complete shift of the American view of the role of government. *Government* under Roosevelt, and particularly the Executive, was to be all-powerful. The defense of this—if there was a defense—was that the people freely and frequently could pass judgment upon it. As long as there were free elections at stated times, there could not be overpowering objection to such a government. In protection of the people—that is, in this case the minority—against the possible action of such a government, the strong weapon in American practice was free speech and the free press. Any suppression of absolute freedom would tend to limit the field of criticism.

Franklin Roosevelt was credited by millions with being their savior. Yet, on the whole, this leadership—in method and result—was injurious to the slow working of democracy as Americans know it, and have thought of it in terms of the leadership of Jefferson or Lincoln or Wilson.

Dependence upon continuous consultation with unofficial advisers, upon acceptable compromise, and finally an arbitrary and personal decision—are characteristic of a tribal chieftain's point of view. But it was limited in value in a world of developed science and knowledge. It was "Politics."

The President who would deal with "kings" and who was surrounded by the men "of his court," and who could advise and counsel with many, must also gather from many sources the intellectual content of his pronouncements. As this practice grew, the habit of dependence upon conferences tended to dictate Mr. Roosevelt's direction of the policies of the United States.

Even before actual war came upon the United States, there was outstanding example of a determination of the actual direction of the American people, without their consent, in his proclamation of the Atlantic Charter.

On the deck of a warship surrounded not by the chosen representatives of the people, but by his personal advisers and selected representatives of the army and the navy, he proclaimed the principles—as he saw them—that would cause the United States to enter upon a course that eventually led to involvement in war. As a platform for a group glorifying in the might of America for the righteous cause of all humanity, it was superb.

Military conquerors have high place in the annals of the race, and military leaders have been given high place even by the people of the United States. A basic reason rests in the acceptance of conflict as the primary condition of all mankind. Political leaders make it their chief concern to channel these conflicts into peaceful discussions and acceptable decisions.

Statesmen are those who, because of mental superiority, moral conviction, and energetic activity, provide peaceful victories. But no statesman, and certainly no political leader, has for the mass of mankind the hold upon the imagination that is accorded the conqueror. It is so easy to see what the conqueror does, so hard to judge what the statesman accomplishes.

Franklin Roosevelt presented himself to his people as a leader in conflicts in which they had deep interest. This was accompanied by praise of their accomplishments as they saw them. He fought the selfish "interests" that had engulfed the nation in ruin; he fought the political forces that stood across the path of the popular will; he fought the totalitarian rulers that would dominate the world. (As Commander-in-Chief he came to his full powers.)

Mistakes in military leadership may be traced directly to Mr. Roosevelt as Commander-in-Chief. Careful distinctions must, however, be made. The United States was plunged into World War II by a military defeat of first magnitude. Ever since the Japanese attack on Pearl Harbor, the American people in accepting the challenge to united effort, nevertheless questioned the seeming inevitability of that defeat. Some said that a political leader of great acumen, by means of legitimate diplomacy, had forced the enemy to attack first and by so doing, united the American people in support of Presidential policies. Others insisted, without the support of adequate evidence, that the defeat at Pearl Harbor came about through default by President Roosevelt and his military leaders.

The declaration for "unconditional surrender," however circumscribed by American military commanders, even though in part repudiated by the President near the close of the war, was a blunder of first magnitude. It stiffened every resistance and gave tremendous power to the extremists in Germany.

The initial approval of the Morgenthau plan was again a blunder that brought consequences of tremendous cost. It not only gave the German government additional reason for calling for continued resistance; it indicated a blindness to the facts in the case on the part of the American Commander-in-Chief. Such a plan, if adopted, even in part, would strengthen the power of Russia in central Europe and make certain future triumphs for communism.

The crowning mistake in the leadership of Franklin Roosevelt was neither insistence upon unconditional surrender, nor the intended devastation of Germany. A profound misconception of the international situation and an overwhelming belief in the efficacy of a new idealism to change the deep currents of world history led to a persistent attempt to make war serve a definite military result. This was defeat of the enemy without heed to the direct and immediate political result. Mr. Roosevelt shared a common delusion of his time that Russia, and others, would forsake revolution and concentrate upon progress within the nation, and that the Soviet Union could be controlled within the United Nations Organization.

On the other hand, had President Roosevelt as Commander-in-Chief fought the war in terms of collective internationalism, using corresponding methods, he would have been able to establish a union of peoples with great strength. But nationalism was stressed throughout the conduct of the war. This dilemma in time became manifest.

To win the objectives of the war, as he stated them to the American people, the President must in the end construct a means of international agreement, long an American dream but never an American practice. The dream faded, even though the form of belief was provided in the United Nations, for no dominant internationalism appeared. Nationalism emerged stronger than ever, because it had won the war.

Had the President comprehended the international situation as visualized in his own State Department, he might have listened to Churchill even at Yalta. "From some points of view," wrote an official of the State Department charged with responsibility in negotiations preliminary to the San Francisco Conference of United Nations, "the worst feature about this war is that it leaves one or two [nations] face to face with almost no pivot state between. . . . The fateful choice we have taken is to turn aside from what seemed the inevitable pyramidic structure of peoples finally under one power through conquest—which was for long, it seemed, the inevitable outcome of the military age we have lived in to date—to a combination of powers, acting on the principle of agreed forms of restraint and working with other states, in an international organization. This course has been chosen deliberately by the great powers concerned as the alternative to another war in which it would be almost if not actually impossible for one to contend successfully with the other without ruining itself and failing to gain a victory even so."

Everyone has agreed that Mr. Roosevelt must be measured first of all as a world leader. He many times made it clear that he thought so. His era was a time of world tensions—and no amount of preoccupation with national concerns could make it otherwise.

An underlying weakness of his leadership lay in his acceptance of the pragmatic approach to the solution of both domestic and foreign problems. In essence, it was a refusal to take the stand for a distinctively American approach to the basic problems of capitalism. No political program that emerged in the Roosevelt administration was distinctly the expression of the American tradition. In the course of twelve years, at home and abroad, the President stood with the radicals, using the political party parlance of the "middle way" in both instances.

He would extend into the organization of the proposed United Nations the same alignments which he had done so much to strengthen in the United States. Naturally, therefore, he and his immediate advisers would favor the weakening and eventual downfall of all colonialism, of all so-called imperialism, and of the forces of capitalism that in Britain as well as America had built the modern world.

The persuasive ability that Mr. Roosevelt had so constantly used in domestic and in foreign affairs was based upon a willingness to consult and to compromise in the hope of preserving democracy. Having, in truth, no fundamental conviction of the importance of adhering absolutely to Constitutional government as Americans had known it, he likewise saw no necessity of constantly opposing the Communist as well as the Fascist enemies of that philosophy of society. Lack of conviction made it possible for him to assure himself and his followers that he had, in the pragmatic approach, the key to the future.

The recurrent theme of the period 1933-1945 is one of deepest tragedy among the people of the world—a long series of mournful events accompanied by loss of millions of human lives by human violence. The villains in this tragedy were clearly marked. Yet, as clearly, there emerged a hero, a man of good intention who would battle the forces of evil and win. Again and again Franklin Roosevelt won the battle, but in the end he seemed to lose the war. Losing, he was still a hero, but his effort emphasized the tragedy.

Frustration is the result of an attempt to understand this tragedy. Talent he possessed—genius, let it be admitted—in sensing the needs and results of leadership. But did Roosevelt have a real grasp of leadership in ideas, in probing the unknown for answers in the social, economic and political fields? Again and again it would seem that only one immune to real learning and utterly unconscious of the intricacies and complexities of long-sustained argument could blithely assert as Mr. Roosevelt so often did that a solution had been found or was to be found.

By all tests he was a successful politician, the most successful of his day, if what is meant thereby is the manipulation of men, organizations, and programs to the end that the politician and his followers may remain in power. This was all-important if the politician was to take office away from the conservative and keep it out of the hands of the radical. Such a politician, in the course of his ceaseless activity, does accomplish much good, arouse much enthusiasm, and bring to his support millions.

But in terms of the ultimate solution of problems, or of placing such problems in the general stream of American development, he does incalculable harm. The American people accepted the pattern which was gradually woven by Roosevelt's leadership, and on the face of things millions profited from his action. But as the years passed, it became evident that the balance had to be paid. . . .

*   *   *

Franklin Delano Roosevelt appeared in a great role on a vast stage, a hero not only to millions of his fellow countrymen, but also to millions of his contemporaries throughout the world. The role was tragic in a fateful drama—a man of fundamentally good intention overwhelmed by the forces of his time in a gigantic struggle to solve the pressing problems of his nation and of the world. President Roosevelt was a leader in a revolution at home and abroad. The revolution at home was a rearrangement of social and economic forces and a change of the function of government in American life. The revolution abroad was an attempt to substitute for the forces expressed in balance of power among nations the concept of international union to insure peace. The means he used, at home and abroad, to implement his ideas appear in terms of their development under his skillful and adroit direction. The struggle in the final analysis seems to be primarily one of intellectual grasp and moral discrimination. Roosevelt's failure lay in his unsuccessful attempt to justify the means or establish the ends he had in view. This was his personal tragedy. Inasmuch as on major decisions he had a majority support, it was also the tragedy of the American people.[8]

JOHN GUNTHER: FDR, SYMBOL OF THE COMMON MAN

One of the best broad, general and impressionistic efforts to assess FDR's role in history is the portrait attempted by John Gunther. The following short excerpt bears directly on the appraisal of FDR's greatness, but perhaps raises more questions than it answers.

Franklin Delano Roosevelt, thirty-second President of the United States and Chief Executive from 1933 to 1945, the architect of the New Deal and the director of victory in World War II, Franklin Delano Roosevelt who is still both loved and hated as passionately as if he were still alive, was born in Hyde Park, New York, in 1882, and died in Warm Springs, Georgia, in 1945. It was his fate, through what concentration of forces no man can know, to be President during both the greatest depres-

[8] Edgar E. Robinson, *The Roosevelt Leadership* (Philadelphia, 1955), pp. 391-408.

sion and the greatest war the world has ever known. He was a cripple—and he licked them both.

Was he a great man? Of course. But what made him so? How did the greatness arise? His career, by almost any criterion, is one of the most extraordinary in modern times. But exactly why? What controlled his character? What did Roosevelt himself contribute to his own proliferating destiny? What transformed him from a not very exceptional young man into a mature colossus? What came from the *Zeitgeist,* what from him?

I once heard it said that Roosevelt's most effective quality was receptivity. But also he transmitted. He was like a kind of universal joint, or rather a switchboard, a transformer. The whole energy of the country, the whole power of one hundred and forty million people, flowed into him and through him; he not only felt this power, but he utilized it, he retransmitted it. Why does a country, if lucky, produce a great man when he is most needed? Because it really believes in something and focuses the entire energy of its national desires into a single human being; the supreme forces of the time converge into a single vessel. Roosevelt could manipulate this power, shooting it out at almost any angle, to provoke response, to irradiate ideas and men, to search out enormous issues. He was like a needle, always quivering, oscillating, responding to new impulses, throbbing at the slightest variation in current—a magnetic instrument measuring ceaselessly the tone and intensity of public impact. But no matter how much the needle quivered and oscillated, it seldom varied far from its own true north.

But this analysis, however suggestive, is too artificial for my taste, because the essence of F.D.R. was not mechanistic, but sublimely (and sometimes ridiculously) human. Of all his multifarious qualities the dominant was probably his extreme humanity. Later we shall try to break this term down; suffice it to say now that, being a man, he believed in men. The term "humanity" covers a wide arc—from amiability to compassion, from fertility in ideas to subtlety in personal relationships, from the happy expression of animal vitality to the deepest cognizance of suffering and primitive despair. The President was inveterately personal, and people were inveterately personal about him. A lady I know, by no means a sentimentalist, said two or three years after his death, "He made me glad I am a woman. I miss him actively, personally, every day." At least a dozen people all over the country told me early in 1945—the remark became almost trite—"I never met him, but I feel as if I had lost my greatest friend."

His radiant, energetic smile—even with the touch of glucose in it, even when it seemed contrived—stirred people with confidence and hope. His lustrous voice, so soothing, so resonant, so alive, said, "My friends . . ." —and the people were. They were not merely his followers, but partners. He led by following, which was one of the most distinctive sources of his power. He lifted people above themselves—he gave them a goal—and hence no one was ever able to take the masses away from him. He gave citizens the sense that they, we, the country, were going forward, that life was still the kind of adventure it had been in pioneer days, that the pace was fast and that substantial rewards were attainable.

Yet, more than any modern president, he split the country—which is one of the more obvious Roosevelt paradoxes. Why was he hated so, defamed and calumniated so? Because he took from the rich and gave to the poor. But that is only one explanation. Why, five years after his death, is he still hated so? Because what he did lives after him. But that too is only part of the story.

Roosevelt stood for the "common man" (though this ambiguous phrase is a cliché earnestly to be avoided) but he was certainly not common himself. In fact he was a storybook Prince Charming, a fairytale hero to the millions; he ruled with a wand—even if it was an ivory cigarette holder. Out in the rain, men and women strove—literally—to touch the hem of his cape as he passed, this man who could not walk. The "common" people chose him, a prince, to lead them, and he did things for them, as a good prince should. What was the New Deal except a vast exercise in *noblesse oblige?* [9]

To a supreme degree Roosevelt had five qualifications for statesmanship: (a) courage; (b) patience, and an infinitely subtle sense of timing; (c) the capacity to see the very great in the very small, to relate the infinitesimal particular to the all-embracing general; (d) idealism, and a sense of fixed objectives; (e) ability to give resolution to the minds of men. Also he had plenty of bad qualities—dilatoriness, two-sidedness (some critics would say plain dishonesty), pettiness in some personal relationships, a cardinal lack of frankness (for which, however, there was often good reason), inability to say No, love of improvisation, garrulousness, amateurism, and what has been called "cheerful vindictiveness." Amateurism?—in a peculiar way, yes. But do not forget that he was the most masterfully expert practical politician ever to function in this republic.

[9] "A good many writers on FDR have used this *noblesse oblige* analogy, but it should not be pushed too far. Certainly the early New Dealers themselves never thought of the New Deal in *noblesse oblige* terms, nor, I think, did Roosevelt himself. They thought in terms of emergency and social justice." (Gunther footnote.)

I have said that "of course" he was a great man. He fulfilled a concrete historical function, his career epitomized the cardinal pressures of his era, he was what Emerson might have called a Yea-Sayer, a world-man, and no erosion by history will ever efface some of the things he did. He was admired and loved all over the world, not just in the United States; his appeal was universal.

Yet it is difficult to summarize in a single word what he stood for, as one may say that Socrates stood for Reason or Napoleon for Conquest. In a sense Roosevelt was an instrument, not a creator. He was not a true Original. He was not pure, like Joan of Arc, nor profound, like Dante, nor did he breathe fire, like Shelley. He had plenty of moral grandeur, but he was multiplex and multiform. He was neither a poet, a philosopher, an artist, a mystic, nor even an intellectual. He had few Ideas. In sheer brain power, he was outweighed by several of his contemporaries, and somehow he lacked wholeness of soul, in the way that St. Augustine, let us say, had wholeness of soul, or, on a different level, Cromwell or Spinoza. He called himself a Christian and a democrat, but one does not associate with him the overwhelming, overpowering creative impulse that comes to a man with a permanent, absolute devotion to a single principle. Roosevelt was never a man obsessed. He was not a Goethe, whose whole career may be crystallized by the use of a single word, Nature, or even a Gladstone (Liberalism), or a Bismarck (Prussia).

Probably what it all boils down to is the matter of contribution. He did not create a country, as did Masaryk, nor a continent of the imagination, like Beethoven, nor a new world of science, like Freud. He may not have been as stupendous a human being as, say, Michelangelo or Tolstoi, but if you measure a man practically by the work he leaves, FDR ranks very high. A Roosevelt advocate might say: (1) Almost singlehanded he saved democracy in the United States; (2) he brought the United States to world leadership for the first time. Certainly he belongs in the category of Washington and Lincoln as one of the three greatest presidents in American history, whether you like all he did or not. And think how he is missed! [10]

Roosevelt was a man of his times, and what times they were!—chaotic, catastrophic, revolutionary, epochal—he was President during the greatest emergency in the history of mankind, and he never let history—or mankind—down. His very defects reflected the unprecedented strains and stresses of the decades he lived in. But he took history in his stride; he had vision and gallantry enough, oomph and zip and debonair benevo-

[10] John Gunther, *Roosevelt in Retrospect* (New York, 1950), pp. 3-6.

lence enough, to foresee the supreme crises of our era, overcome them, and lead the nation out of the worst dangers it has ever faced.

Roosevelt was the greatest political campaigner and the greatest vote getter in American history. Thirty-one out of forty-eight states voted for him each of the four times he ran. His influence, far from having diminished since his death, has probably increased. When Mr. Truman won his surprising victory in 1948, which was made possible in part by the political influence left behind by FDR, it was altogether fitting that a London newspaper should head its story, "Roosevelt's Fifth Term."

Roosevelt believed in social justice—and fought for it—he gave hope and faith to the masses, and knew that the masses are the foundation of American democracy. He turned the cornucopia of American resource upside down and made it serve almost everybody. Mrs. Roosevelt has said that in the whole course of his career there was never any deviation from his original objective—"to make life better for the average man, woman, and child." I have heard men of the utmost sober conservatism say that they think FDR saved the country from overt revolution in 1932. He created the pattern of the modern democratic state, and made it function. To be a reformer alone is not enough. A reformer must make reform effective. This certainly Roosevelt did. Yet, as we have pointed out, he was a conservative as well as a liberal; he believed in free enterprise and the profit system. It is not beyond the bounds of possibility that thirty or forty years from now the country will have swung so much further left that what FDR stood for will be thought of as almost reactionary.

Also Roosevelt's career nicely disproves an essential constituent of Marxism, namely the principle of class war. His entire life refutes the Marxist thesis. He was a rich man and an aristocrat; but he did more for the underpossessed than any American who ever lived. Moreover, as we know, FDR always operated within the framework of full democracy and civil liberties. He believed devoutly in the American political tradition. Much of the world outside the United States during his prodigious administrations had political liberty without economic security; some had security but no liberty. He gave both.

Mr. Roosevelt was the greatest war president in American history; it was he, almost singlehanded, who created the climate of the nation whereby we were able to fight at all. Beyond this he brought the United States to full citizenship in the world as a partner in the peace. He set up the frame in which a durable peace might have been written and a new world order established; if he had lived to fill in the picture contemporary history might be very different.

Above all FDR was an educator. He expanded and enlarged the role of the Presidency as no president before him ever did. "The first duty of a statesman is to educate," he said in his Commonwealth Club speech back in 1932. He established what amounted to a new relationship between president and people; he turned the White House into a teacher's desk, a pulpit; he taught the people of the United States how the operations of government might be applied to their own good; he made government a much abler process, on the whole, than it has ever been before; he gave citizens intimate acquaintanceship with the realities of political power, and made politics the close inalienable possession of the man in every street.

One result of all this is that the President, though dead, is still alive. Millions of Americans will continue to vote for Roosevelt as long as *they* live.[11]

[11] *Ibid.*, pp. 378-379.

Afterword: FDR in History

What leads us to consider a man great? It is evident that each generation, and each society develops differing criteria. But certainly the range and the diversity of one man's influence on his own and on succeeding generations is one measure. Great individuals often play a large number of different roles and their impact may be many-sided. FDR, for example, played a variety of roles and reflected the varied characteristics of American society. Perhaps this explains why there was so much controversy among contemporaries and among later biographers over his place in history, since each tended to focus upon one particular aspect of his personality. But it was his ability to assume so many different functions of national leadership concurrently which enabled him to exert such a great influence upon contemporaries during his lifetime.

FDR tended to think more of his immediate functions rather than of his long range role. As President, thus, he saw his prime responsibility was to deal with the crisis of depression. This might have been done by utilizing all of the existing powers available to a Chief Executive—as both Theodore Roosevelt and Woodrow Wilson had done so brilliantly. However, FDR's strong executive leadership was reflected in the creation of dozens of new federal agencies designed to *bypass* existing departments. He also interpreted his constitutional mandate as entitling him to the mantle of a legislative leader, for much of the legislation during the New Deal received its impetus from the White House. In addition, as a long-time advocate of judicial reform, he attempted to impose a certain measure of executive pressure upon the federal judiciary, although his efforts to secure reorganization of the United States Supreme Court in 1937 miscalculated the public's sentiment. But his varied activities in dealing with the depression indicate—together with his own statements—that he saw his role as that of a strong President who in a time of national crisis made full use of the powers granted him under the Constitution.

Unlike many of his critics, FDR also considered himself as a conservator of traditional American values. As his son, James,[1] noted, few men were

---

[1] Reference, for scholarly and personal criticisms in the Afterword, should be made to the Bibliographical Note.

more closely wedded to American values and institutions than his father. Thus FDR never quite understood the accusations of those who accused him of undermining American democracy. Instead, he frequently alluded to the policies of the United States elaborated during the American Revolution, the Jeffersonian era, the reform era of Theodore Roosevelt and Woodrow Wilson, in order to emphasize his view that others before him had taken what had seemed like drastic measures to preserve fundamental American freedoms. His function, as he saw it, was to undertake another of those periodic overhaulings of the American system, not unlike several others which it had undergone during the previous one hundred and fifty years.

In the realm of diplomacy FDR tended to assume the role of an educator. Until World War II one of his prime objectives was to awaken Americans to the dangers of isolationism in the face of danger from aggressor nations, and to secure greater acceptance of the principle of international cooperation as a means of safeguarding the nation's security. Certainly FDR grasped the German and Japanese designs several years before the majority of the American public, and his speeches and other public statements after 1937 reflect his effort to awaken Americans to these realities.

Contemporary observers saw FDR in still other roles, their views, however, usually tinged with a measure of emotionalism. To Europeans he appeared to be the Savior of Democracy at a time when totalitarian governments were springing up throughout the world. As Sir Isaiah Berlin reflected, it was FDR who revitalized the processes of democratic government to show the world that democracy could deal with pressing economic and social problems at least as effectively as other forms of government, and without necessarily surrendering political freedoms.

Others viewed FDR as a national "morale booster." Those who lived during the depression decade, like Frances Perkins, frequently noticed FDR's spirit of optimism, which infected the entire nation. In his personal contacts, in his press conferences and radio addresses, and in his general approach to problems, FDR revealed a personal hopefulness which revived the hopes of millions who were despairing. He restored confidence not only in the American political and economic system, but, perhaps more importantly, in individuals themselves.

To the millions of people who knew his voice, FDR seemed to be a personal friend. The thousands of letters which poured into the White House reflected the *rapport* which FDR was able to establish with large numbers of people who actually never had direct, personal contact with him. To them he seemed a friend and confidante, a man who could be trusted to do his best with the numerous difficulties which plagued almost everyone during the Depression.

Finally, certain contemporaries saw FDR primarily as the Father of the New Deal. In later years historians were to explain in detail that many of the measures of the Roosevelt Administration had numerous precedents or that FDR himself really deserved no credit or blame for the important reforms of his period. FDR's reluctance to support the Wagner Act is a case in point. But to contemporaries it seemed as if almost every action of the federal government during the Roosevelt Era emanated from the President himself. Whether they loved him or hated him, many Americans saw FDR as a symbol of all that was good or bad in the New Deal.

Contemporaries were less sure of FDR's role in foreign policy than in domestic affairs. They found it difficult to discern a course of clear action on his part and considered him largely as an improvisor. Defenders of FDR, such as William L. Langer, have noted that FDR was hampered in his diplomacy by the force of public opinion. Perhaps this is why some observers, especially his close associate, Sumner Welles, found him more or less reflecting public sentiment in the shifting diplomatic policies of the New Deal.

When historians began to assess the dimensions of FDR's personality, they discovered him playing still other roles. Arthur Schlesinger, Jr., and others, regarded FDR as the personification of American liberalism, as the twentieth century Jeffersonian disciple. In their view, FDR used modern methods to implement eighteenth century democratic ideals such as equality and democracy. In this role he was the natural carrier of the Progressive tradition, and the heir of Theodore Roosevelt and Woodrow Wilson.

Some writers, Mario Einaudi among them, have seen FDR as the father of the welfare state in the United States. Unlike Herbert Hoover, who believed that government bore no responsibility for the welfare of the individual, FDR felt that local, state, and federal authorities had a duty to maintain minimum standards for social and economic well being. Above all, every American had a right to employment and to an adequate wage which the federal government should guarantee. Within the context of prevailing American values, this seemed to imply a significant change of attitudes and practices in the relationship of the government to the individual. FDR helped to effect the new conception through measures such as the WPA, the Wagner Act, the Social Security Act, the

Fair Labor Standards Act, and attempted national health legislation. Those who for good or ill seek the origins of the welfare state in America frequently point to FDR as its progenitor in modern form.

In the field of foreign affairs many historians have viewed FDR as the Apostle of Internationalism. Langer and Gleason especially have pointed to his efforts to implement national defense after 1937 in order to deter German and Japanese aggression. His development of an informal alliance with Great Britain after Munich in 1938 showed his strong belief in collective security. Certainly he became the most influential spokesman for the cause of the democracies within the United States.

During World War II FDR had still other functions. Military historians, such as Maurice Matloff, and others, have focussed on FDR's role as Commander-in-Chief of the armed forces, and the manifold decisions which he was compelled to make in this capacity. These responsibilities brought out additional qualities of leadership in the President which he had not displayed in earlier years.

To many diplomatic historians, such as Herbert Feis, perhaps FDR's most important role was leader of the United Nations and the free world during the war. In this capacity FDR provided inspiration for the Allied populations everywhere. In his person he seemed to embody the hopes and ideals for which millions were striving, whether these included social equality, economic opportunity, or political liberty. Whichever aspect of American society oppressed individuals admired, in FDR they often saw a hope for its realization.

Very likely the meanings which men have found—and will find—in the life of FDR have not been exhausted. Future generations will discover still other roles which FDR filled which will have meaning and significance for them. Perhaps it was a measure of his greatness that he was able to appeal to so many different yearnings in human beings of every nationality and background. But then, the discovery of greatness is not merely a task for the great individual himself, or for his contemporaries, or even for later historians, but for every person who is in some way affected by great works and deeds.

Bibliographical Note

The literature concerning FDR is voluminous, if of uneven quality. Students and the general reader who wish to acquaint themselves with FDR's own writings, with accounts by his contemporaries, and those of later critics, should find a representative collection in most university and public libraries. They may also wish to make a visit to the Franklin D. Roosevelt Library at Hyde Park, New York, to view the Roosevelt home and the museum there. The Library also houses the FDR manuscripts, and the collections of his close associates, such as Louis Howe, are also available for inspection.

Among the more useful bibliographies of materials bearing on the life of FDR, see E. E. Robinson, *The Roosevelt Leadership, 1933-1945* (Philadelphia, 1955), pp. 411-480, and Frank Freidel, "The New Deal, 1929-1941," in *Yearbook of the National Council for the Social Studies,* Vol. XXXI (1961). A highly selective, but useful list is in James M. Burns, *Roosevelt: The Lion and the Fox,* ed. Harbinger (New York, 1956), pp. 493-538.

FDR's life in his own words can be followed in Elliot Roosevelt, ed., *F.D.R.: His Personal Letters* (4 vols., New York, 1947-1950), which emphasizes his personal rather than his public life. The latter, as reflected in speeches, press conferences, and public pronouncements has been most ably illuminated in Samuel Rosenman, ed., *The Public Papers and Addresses of Franklin D. Roosevelt* (13 vols., New York, 1938-1950). More selective collections of his speeches include Franklin D. Roosevelt, *Looking Forward* (New York, 1933), and *On Our Way* (New York, 1934), which recapture some of the atmosphere of this exciting and trying period. Before 1933 FDR also wrote short pieces for magazines and newspapers, and some of the best of these efforts have been collected in D. S. Carmichael, ed., *F.D.R.: Columnist* (Chicago, 1947).

Many informal remarks by FDR when President were gathered by one of his close aides, William Hassett, in *Off the Record with FDR, 1942-1945* (New Brunswick, 1958). Although the bulk of FDR's correspondence is in the manuscript collections of the Franklin D. Roosevelt Library, certain portions have been published. Carroll Kilpatrick has edited *Roosevelt and Daniels* (Chapel Hill, 1952), which contains many interesting letters between FDR and his former chief in the Navy Department during World War I, and which focusses on the personal life of FDR. A more formal interchange can be found in *Wartime Correspondence of Pius XII and Franklin Delano Roosevelt* (New York, 1947), edited by Myron C. Taylor.

In addition, some useful collections of FDR's statements have been made. These include Donald Day, ed., *FDR's Own Story* (Boston, 1951), which encompasses selections from public and from private papers. A similar compilation with greater emphasis on FDR's public life is by Basil Rauch, ed., *The Roosevelt Reader* (New York, 1957). A volume which also contains writings of FDR's contemporaries in addition to his own is by James N. Rosenau, ed., *The Roosevelt Treasury* (Garden City, 1951). Its topical arrangement of FDR's career enhances its usefulness for the beginning student. Of shorter compass is Karl Schriftgiesser's "Franklin Delano Roosevelt: a Self-Portrait," in *The New York Times Magazine*, March 26, 1950, p. 13 ff. FDR's life can be followed in pictures in Stefan Lorant, ed., *FDR: a Pictorial Biography* (New York, 1950).

Hundreds of FDR's contemporaries have left accounts of their impressions of him. Some of the most important are by members of his family, especially Eleanor Roosevelt, in *This is My Story* (New York, 1937), and *This I Remember* (New York, 1949). Some insight into FDR's public career can be gathered from Elliott Roosevelt, *As He Saw It* (New York, 1949); and James Roosevelt emphasizes human aspects of the family relationships in *Affectionately, FDR* (New York, 1958).

FDR's Cabinet members and others who worked in the Administration have left revealing memoirs reflecting diverse aspects of his personality. One of the fullest and most perceptive of these appraisals is by Rexford Tugwell in *The Democratic Roosevelt* (Garden City, 1957), which has considerable information about FDR's political skills. A warm remembrance reiterating FDR's human qualities is by Frances Perkins, *The Roosevelt I Knew* (New York, 1946), which is a highly favorable account. Not quite so full of adulation is a book by the disillusioned former Brain Truster, Raymond Moley—*After Seven Years* (New York, 1939), which is invaluable for an understanding of the inner workings of the early New Deal. Less informative is James F. Byrnes, *Speaking Frankly* (New York, 1947), although it contains some good sections dealing with World War II diplomacy. Harold L. Ickes in *The Secret Diary of Harold L. Ickes* (3 vols., New York, 1953-1954) is highly opinionated, but indispensible for a complete view of FDR. Among FDR's Cabinet members, Henry L. Morgenthau was often closest to him, and thus John M. Blum, ed., *From the Morgenthau Diaries, Years of Crisis, 1928-1938* (Boston, 1959) cannot be ignored. Morgenthau was also antagonistic to Ickes and thus his diaries provide a good corrective to those of Ickes. Alben Barkley in *That Reminds Me* (Garden City, 1954), and Tom Connally and Alfred Steinberg in *My Name is Tom Connally* (New York, 1954), provide a glimpse of FDR as he looked from the halls of Congress. Some disgruntled New Dealers have left accounts of their experiences, notably Hugh S. Johnson in *The Blue Eagle-from Egg to Earth* (Garden City, 1935), and Donald Richberg in *My Hero* (New York, 1954).

Some lesser assistants around FDR have written memoirs. These include Secret Service agents and personal aides such as Michael F. Reilly (with William J. Slocum), *Reilly of the White House* (New York, 1947), Ross T. McIntire, *White House Physician* (New York, 1946), and Grace Tully, FDR's former secretary, in *FDR, My Boss* (New York, 1949). A more distant view by a dean of the Washington press corps is A. Merriman Smith's *Thank You, Mr. President* (New York, 1946). Less important is Walter Tittle's *Roosevelt as an Artist Saw Him* (New York, 1948).

A number of notable contemporary observers left their impressions of FDR as a diplomatist. Perhaps the most important is Winston S. Churchill in *The Gathering Storm* (Boston, 1948), *Their Finest Hour* (Boston, 1949), *The Grand Alliance* (Boston, 1950), and *The Hinge of Fate* (Boston, 1950). Just as notable is Cordell Hull, *The Memoirs of Cordell Hull* (2 vols., New York, 1948), and Henry L. Stimson and McGeorge Bundy in their volume, *On Active Service in Peace and War* (New York, 1948). Also useful is Sumner Welles' *The Time for Decision* (New York, 1944), and Edward R. Stettinius Jr.'s *Roosevelt and the Russians* (New York, 1949). Much less informative is William D. Leahy, *I Was There* (New York, 1950). More distant views are by Dwight D. Eisenhower, in his *Crusade in Europe* (New York, 1948), and Joseph W. Stilwell in *The Stilwell Papers,* ed. Theodore H. White (New York, 1948).

Later biographers and historians have filled literally thousands of books while seeking to make an estimate of FDR. Background materials on FDR's family can be found in Herman Hagedorn's *The Roosevelt Family of Sagamore Hill* (New York, 1954), and more specifically with reference to FDR in Karl Schriftgiesser's *The Amazing Roosevelt Family* (New York, 1942).

In addition to the multi-volume standard biography of FDR by Frank Freidel, and the one-volume life by James M. Burns, there are several general surveys of FDR's presidential years. These include a very broad and simple work intended for the general reader by Denis W. Brogan, *The Era of Franklin Delano Roosevelt* (New Haven, 1950). Dexter Perkins has also written a simple and general account in *The New Age of Franklin Roosevelt, 1932-1945* (Chicago, 1957), with an emphasis on political and diplomatic events. A not very successful effort to make a psychological appraisal of FDR is by Noel F. Busch in *What Manner of Man* (New York, 1944). A vitriolic estimate of FDR is in John T. Flynn's *Country Squire in the White House* (New York, 1940).

Many of the more serious studies of FDR focus on a particular aspect of his career. These include Bernard Bellush in *Franklin D. Roosevelt as Governor of New York* (New York, 1958), Daniel Fusfeld in *The Economic Thought of Franklin D. Roosevelt* (New York, 1955), and Harold Gosnell in *Champion Campaigner: Franklin D. Roosevelt* (New York, 1952). Focussing as much on his policies as on his personality are Mario Einaudi's *The Roosevelt Revolution* (New York, 1959), a highly appreciative study of FDR, and E. E. Robinson's *The Roosevelt Leadership, 1932-1945* (Philadelphia, 1955), which finds FDR sadly wanting in most aspects of statesmanship. Because Louis M. Howe, FDR's most important aide, was closer to his chief than any other man, the work by Alfred B. Rollins, *Roosevelt and Howe* (New York, 1964), is indispensible for an understanding of FDR.

A number of outstanding works discuss FDR's role in foreign affairs. William L. Langer and S. Everett Gleason in *The World Crisis and American Foreign Policy* (2 vols., New York: 1952-1953) deal extensively with FDR's policies. Herbert Feis in *The Road to Pearl Harbor* (Princeton,

1950) does the same in a somewhat briefer compass. Charles A. Beard made a bitter indictment of FDR's diplomacy in *President Roosevelt and the Coming of the War 1941* (New Haven, 1948), which Basil Rauch sought to answer in *Roosevelt: From Munich to Pearl Harbor* (New York, 1950). A representative group of selections from books with divergent viewpoints concerning FDR's role at Yalta is in Richard Fenno, ed., *The Yalta Conference* (Boston, 1955).

Index